To Aimee R. Su,

My oldest friend and companion,

who still possesses the beauty of Berber,

the will of Droste

➤❧ NOTE TO THE READER ❧◀

When Anita Berber's remarkably short and tragic career came to an abrupt end in November 1928, both her critics and devotees saw the dancer's death as a cautionary tale about the beginnings of their own era. Anita represented an artistic generation that defied any and all restraints. The wild hedonism and frenetic theatrics of her early post-World War I years seemed to parallel Germany's descent into communal madness.

By the time Anita was buried, however, most German historians thought their nation had finally stabilized into a prosperous, stable democracy. Few could have predicted the period of economic collapse, radical political infighting, and Nazi rule that would soon follow.

The Seven Addictions and Five Professions of Anita Berber is the story of Weimar's first stage. Within this Anita Berber biography are separate chapters on the Naked Dance ("Dance in the New Nineveh"), the further adventures of her second husband Sebastian Droste ("Exit Baron Von Droste"), and a translation of Droste and Berber's 1922 book *The Dances of Depravity, Horror, and Ecstasy.*

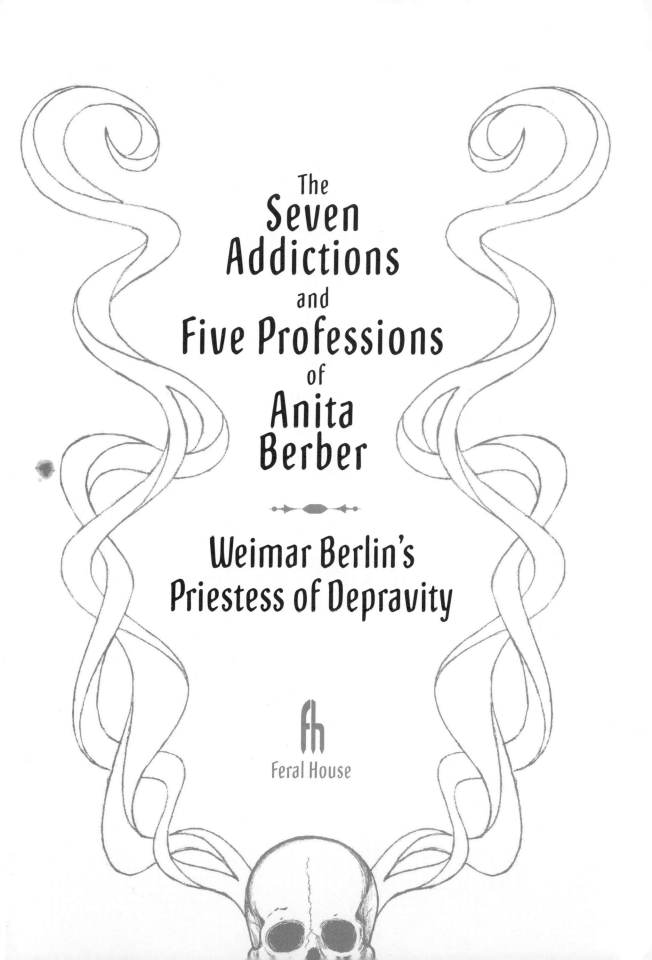

The
Seven
Addictions
and
Five Professions
of
Anita
Berber

Weimar Berlin's
Priestess of Depravity

Feral House

The Seven Addictions and Five Professions of Anita Berber
©2006 by Mel Gordon

ISBN: 1-932595-12-0

10 9 8 7 6 5 4 3 2 1

Feral House
PO Box 39910
Los Angeles, CA 90039
www.feralhouse.com

Design: Sean Tejaratchi

The photographs and drawings in *The Seven Addictions and Five Professions of Anita Berber* come from many published sources and private archives. (Only a small fraction of the dance images were ever properly captioned or identified.) Each illustration has its own history and legal claim. Many were publicity stills or 80-year-old made-for-hire graphics.

The copyright ownership of some photographs today is unclear since they were printed in multiple publications simultaneously, the original creators (or legal retainers) were Jewish—all contracts held by them were deliberately destroyed during the Nazi era—or because of the differing statues in the European Union and the United States regarding the issues of public domain.

The author would like to thank Lothar Fischer for his generosity in making several images available for reproduction in this book.

CONTENTS

INTRODUCTION

Anita Berber was a very beautiful girl and a dancer. And she danced primarily in nightclubs in the nude. If you think what we see now on stage, you know with Broadway's nudity and all, it's like going to a kindergarten, compared to Berber's "Dance of Lust." I loved her too much to call her dirty. She was exotic and strange and that's what made her so special.

—Lotte Lenya on *The Dick Cavett Show*, 1975

On the evening of July 13th, 1928, at the beginning of her solo "Dance in White," Anita Berber collapsed on the cabaret floor of a Beirut tourist dive-bar. A few hours later, a physician at a French-run hospital studied her nearly emaciated body. His diagnosis was direct and unsparing: the 29-year-old German dancer suffered from an advanced state of pulmonary tuberculosis; no therapy or medical treatment was advised. The patient rallied slightly the next day but was informed that she had little time left.

Four months later, Anita Berber was buried in a pauper's grave outside Berlin. Only thrill-seeking transvestite couples from the Eldorado nightclub, some somber journalists and intellectuals in top hats, a couple of film directors, the German sexologist Dr. Magnus Hirschfeld, and immediate relatives from the Berber clan attended. Henri Châtin-Hoffmann, Anita's third husband, an American, and his latest dance partner watched from afar. The intimate and bohemian ceremony that was planned had to be curtailed due to a nonstop rainfall.

It was the end of an era.

Dutch review of one of Anita Berber's last dance recitals in Europe,
Cinema en Theater, **Autumn 1926**

Weimar Berlin's notorious starlet, a "phallic woman," the reincarnation of the cult-goddess Astarte, the avatar of female desire and perversity, had finally succumbed to the stimulants and addictions that made her the single most decadent personality in a world without moral boundaries or legal restriction.

But beyond her reigning status as the signifier of German bad-girl behavior—a "priestess of depravity"—who was this Anita Berber?

To be sure, she was an accomplished Expressionist poet, iconic fashion model, naked dancer, and silent film actress. No description of Berlin during its wildest Inflation years in 1922 and 1923 was complete without a startling Berber anecdote or scandalous reference. Marlene Dietrich rode to fame on Anita Berber's stock-in-trade: the silk-stockinged legs and gentleman-like demeanor. Lotte Lenya

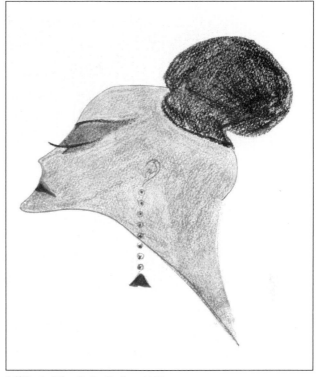

Self-Portrait **by Anita Berber, 1922**

articulated Anita's distinctive sexual ambiguity in song and stage character. Lya da Putti portrayed pouty Amazons and fickle debutantes in evident homage to Berber's stage and film performances. Among Central Europe's countless femme fatales, only Anita Berber was noted for her unvarnished belief in artistic authenticity and her rootless, nearly unquenchable, lust for ineffable sensations.

Whether decked out in male attire or stripped naked, Anita revealed yet another side of her fugitive persona and her dedication to genuine grief and exaltation, to body madness, to unadulterated eroticism. Her dances were the dark manifestations of a shape-shifting desperado.

The men and women within the lost girl's orbit were compelled to borrow shamelessly from her bag of outlaw tricks. Anita's innovations—her scenic coldness, her pansexual revelations, her opaque concoctions of autobiography and artifice—were too appealing to ignore. But none of Anita's gang or her many imitators could tap into the Madonna's unsettled soul or faithfully reproduce her mysterious visions. Even Greta Garbo, who starred in the Oscar-winning film Grand Hotel as a Berber stand-in, failed to capture the disquieting essence of the winsome rebel.

When Anita Berber was interred in Berlin's St. Thomas cemetery, contemporary writers and historians sensed something wondrous had just ceased to exist. It signaled a tectonic, if barely newsworthy, shift in popular European culture, like the disappearance of a minor folk form or the shunting of a once-flourishing religious sect. The doe-eyed German performer was dutifully mourned, evaluated anew in the years following her death, then elevated into the realm of erotic legend.

The Czech dance critic, Joe Jencik, recognized the fable-like significance of the dissipated starlet best in his miniature biography, *Anita Berberová: Studie* (Prague: Terpsichora, 1930): "Anita Berber's long, bony hand ripped the silken dress off the tarted-up old woman—a ghostly figure the dancer called Public Morality. Now they stood in front of one another, each naked with horrible scars. Berber's whip lashed out at the ancient hag: but Anita always punished herself at the very moment when she tore open the doddering whore's repulsive flesh. The two played out an ecstatic dance of human desire and destitution. They fought each other savagely but both of them knew implicitly that the ruination of one was the ultimate death of the other."

CHAPTER ONE
THE MADONNA FROM DRESDEN

(1899–1918)

The Berlin Apollo-Theater awoke to new life when a young female artist appeared on its stage. Her presentation there was a great success. One could see that Anita Berber was already a mature performer. Her dances at the Apollo radiated brilliance on both conceptional and pictorial levels. Her unusually beautiful and tasteful use of costumes astonished —especially in the "Korean Dance." There she produced a harmony of gesture, movement, and costume. Her performance was absolutely exemplary. In that bizarre dance-depiction, the artist's special charm manifested itself strikingly. Remote from everything saccharine, Anita Berber appeared somewhat "boyish." Her tart slim figure managed to portray that image with sensational results.

—*Elegante Welt* #3 (January 31, 1917)

To dance and film critics in the Kaiser's Berlin, Anita Berber projected a dizzying vision of the New Woman. Her strikingly expressive face, androgynous body, precisely executed movements, and revealing costumes manifested a novel aesthetic: the flapper as artist.

Anita also knew how to shatter the rules of theatrical and social convention. The supreme female provocateur of German bourgeois society knew the tastes, prohibitions, and taboos of her audiences unerringly. The Dresden Madonna grew up in their midst. Anita's upbringing in the final years of the Wilhelmian monarchy followed a more or less typical German middle-class route. She experienced little *lumpenprol* anguish or slumlife struggle that characterized the vast majority of her fellow cabaret artistes

Felix Berber

and naked dancers in the interwar Weimar period.

Little is known about Anita Berber's childhood and early adolescence aside from the stories that Leo Lania recorded in his "biographical novel" *Tanz ins Dunkel: Anita Berber* [*Dance in the Dark: Anita Berber*] (Berlin: Adalbert Schultz Verlag, 1929). Lania, a left-wing Viennese journalist and playwright, claimed to have contacted and/or interviewed nearly all of Anita's friends and acquaintances during a six-month period following her death. These included Anita's mother, Lucie Berber; her half-brother Hans Berber-Credner; her lesbian lover and manager, Susi Wanowski; Anita's sometime paramour and protector, Dr. Heinrich Klapper, a disreputable Berlin abortionist; and her third husband, Henri Châtin-Hoffmann, a maniacal dancer-*bon vivant* from Baltimore. Lania himself knew Anita when he was introduced to her in the spring of 1922 and followed her career with unflagging personal dedication.

At the time he was gathering materials on Berber's life, Lania was professionally engaged by Erwin Piscator, the leading German Communist stage director. At the Volksbühne, Lania pioneered a new form of theatrical writing called "Documentary Drama." Also known as the "Living Newspaper," this new genre of playwriting attempted to defictionalize story-telling through a heavy reliance on public transcripts and documented dialogue. *Tanz ins Dunkel* adhered to a similar strategy although Lania's biographical montage frequently altered names and events to fit the format of his popular biography. Thirteen years later, Lania's political autobiography written in exile, *Today We Are Brothers* (Boston: Houghton Mifflin Co., 1942), corrected many of the "facts" that appeared in his 1929 "nonfiction" novel. Taken together, it is still possible to assemble a psychological profile and chronology of Anita Berber's early years.

Anita's father, Felix Berber, a musical Wunderkind from Leipzig, never failed to boast about his lofty position as a first violinist with the Municipal Orchestra. His virtuoso dexterity found supporters from Berlin to Moscow. He was also something of a *Mitteleuropean* Casanova. In Dresden, the feckless and social-climbing cad impregnated Lucie Thiem, then a minor actress and singer. The mismatched pair married in 1899, a few months before Anita was born on June 10th.

Lucie's mother in Dresden raised the free-spirited, red-haired, and severely near-sighted girl. Felix divorced his chanteuse wife in 1901 and moved to Munich, where he wed a professor's daughter (his third of five marriages) and joined his distinguished

Lucie Berber by Atelier Eberth, 1921

new father-in-law at the Music Academy. Four years later, Lucie fled the Saxon hinterland for Berlin, the entertainment colossus of Central Europe. She soon appeared on the revue stage of Rudolf Nelson's Chat Noir cabaret.

❧ CHILDHOOD IN 5/4 TIME ☙

Back in Dresden, Anita enjoyed a materially comfortable but emotionally sterile and solitary childhood. The marital split and double abandonment stigmatized her at school and crippled her ability to bond or form lasting relationships. Physically, Anita was slight and underdeveloped. She constantly and aggressively acted out her parent's desertion, mutilating the faces of her porcelain dolls and even pretending to be the quarry of knife-

Anita with Grandma Thiem, 1901

wielding maniacs. Grandmother Thiem enrolled the troublesome tomboy in the Jaques-Dalcroze Institute, a utopian academy in nearby Hellerau. The progressive institute emphasized psychophysical training and radical revolutionary movement exercise. For the first time, the ten-year-old Anita took to a disciplinary regimen and schooling.

The Dalcroze instructors attempted to instill a sense of complicated percussive rhythms in the bodies of their youthful charges. Arms, legs, and torsos moved independently to the pounding of drums and repeated piano chords. The children's marches, across studio floors and up stairways, appeared to the growing set of observers as virtually superhuman and visually stunning. It formed a novel choreographic aesthetic called Eurhythmics and fell somewhere between dance and abstract acting. Neither folk-dance nor ballet, Dalcroze's corporal vocabulary was based on "natural" and automatic bodily correspondences to primeval musical stimulation.

Eurhythmics taught conscious control over the physical organism. In some aspects it treated the human body like a musical instrument: the arms moved precisely with the beats of the music to indicate measure; the lower torso and legs followed the rhythmic structure of the composition; the upper torso and head responded to the emotional content of the melody. Altogether, there were five phases of Eurhythmic training, involving respiration, gymnastics and rhythmic speech. Essentially, the work was designed to coordinate movement in rhythmic patterns, to eliminate extraneous gesture, to establish a continuous and automatic contact between the brain and limbs. In this way, the participant experienced Dalcroze's dream of "rhythm consciousness."

In her third year at the Dresden gymnasium, the bespectacled Anita fell head over heels for an oafish senior, Heinz Merten. To secure her affections, the 17-year-old boy rifled through the school's soccer cashbox to buy Anita *sachertorts* in the afternoons and plied the impressionable girl with tales of adventure. He promised to take her with him to America (where they would publicly suicide) or explore the Arctic wastelands or make a fortune at the Berlin Borse. But Heinz, under interrogation, confessed to the theft of the missing 50 marks and promised the school officials that he would return to his formerly lawful ways. Anita, now established as a budding dangerous female among the rebellious pupils and freethinking instructors, soon grew tired of her bourgeois Heinz. His lovemaking abilities were thoroughly inadequate, she informed her gossip-mongering girlfriends.

In 1913, Anita was sent to Zapport and then to Weimar to be with Lucie. There, the 14-year-old learned cooking and studied French at an expensive girls' boarding school. She developed a lifelong addiction to pastries and sugary cream concoctions. The sweetness she found lacking at home could be purchased in patisseries and bakeshops in Weimar's Old Town.

The Great War, which broke out in the late summer of 1914, did not impede Anita's schooling or personal ambitions. It only tamped down her sense of adventure. London and Paris were suddenly proclaimed centers of virulent anti-German intrigue, not way stations for international celebrity. In Weimar, French cuisine was replaced by lesser regional fare. Even mayonnaise was rechristened a Central European condiment. The patriotic city of Neoclassicism now promulgated all things Goethean and nominally Aryan.

At the hairdresser's, Anita spied a 23-year-old dentist through a rip in the partition that separated the women's section from the men's. He was blonde and wore a solid gold

Goethe ring on his right hand. Anita pursued him until the handsome Dr. Lang returned the compliment. He proposed marriage.

Lucie countered that no professional dancer could be tied down by such petty matrimonial bounds. The 15-year-old romantic agreed and broke off the wartime engagement. Tossing salads and baking cream puddings was Anita's first career choice but dancing had its attractions as well. The teenage vixen's perfectly tapered legs and arms more than made up for her underdeveloped chest.

In 1915, Anita moved to the grandmother's apartment in Wilmersdorf, outside Berlin. It was a vain attempt to disengage herself from Lucie's rather faint-hearted notions of parental control. Just a few months later, the chanteuse followed her daughter to the family hideaway. Unbeknownst to grandmother or mother, Anita had secretly enrolled at Maria Moissi's private acting class for young women.

Maria, the wife of Max Reinhardt's reigning Shakespearean star, Alexander Moissi, charged anywhere from 10 to 20 marks per hour for private coaching. Her introductory lessons, however, were not up to Anita's professional expectations. The exercises in theatrical deportment were surprisingly amateurishly devised and banal. Worse, the schoolmistress' laconic approach to character development unfolded in an equally mechanical fashion. Anita daydreamed about returning to the beloved Dalcroze work and experimental dance.

One afternoon in the politically sobering winter of 1915, the choreographer Rita Sacchetto appeared at Moissi's studio apartment. She needed a small corps of young female actresses for a public dance concert and proposed to train them in plastic movement. Many of Moissi's pupils were noted for their physical attractiveness and rhythmical strengths. The offering held a strong crossover appeal.

DANCE SCHOOL
❧ RITA SACCHETTO ❧

Like Anita, Rita Sacchetto came from an art music family from the South. Her two brothers achieved considerable renown for their oversized "living paintings"—*tableaux vivants* that graphically portrayed human beings in real-life groupings. Madame Sacchetto staged her first solo dance performance in Munich in 1905. Her artistic specialty, the slowly unfolding of "poses plastiques," combined stationary Isadora-like character attitudes within simple balletic arrangements. Borrowing from the Dalcroze philosophy, each Sacchetto gesture corresponded to a single chord of the musical score.

During the 1909–1910 season, Sacchetto's private recitals appeared on dance halls throughout western Europe and North America. At the New York Metropolitan Opera House, Madame Sacchetto's performance was widely hailed as the latest in avant-garde choreography, a "symphonic dance of the future." It was one of the earliest international displays of *Ausdruckstanz*, the New German Dance.

Exploring the dark mystery of human emotionality, these German movement pioneers presented nearly naked female (as well as androgynous male) forms that were animated by kinesthetic expressions of sexual desire and psychophysical atmospherics. The astonishing freedom of *Ausdruckstanz* sparked a multitude of possibilities in choreographic storytelling and inspired tradition-shattering patterns of pure abstract motion.

Returning to Munich, Sacchetto performed with the Russian ballet sensation Alexander Sacharoff, and in 1915, six months after the German invasion of France, opened her own studio in the Gruenwald precinct of Berlin.

Anita, among the selected coterie from Maria Moissi's studio, was the obvious standout and Rita's favored initiate. The skinny kid from Dresden had finally come into her own. According to the contemporary writer Dinah Nelken, Anita possessed a naïve charm and an undisguised vivaciousness. Sacchetto's three male leads were utterly taken with the flirtatious redhead. Anita's free spirit and newly-minted eroticism added daring élan and an energizing brio to the much-anticipated evening.

Premiering at the prestigious Blüthner-Saal on February 24th, 1916, Rita Sacchetto's troupe enacted both solo and group dance-pictures. Newspaper advertisements listed classical and bacchanal scenes, contemporary waltzes, grotesque parodies, and "Oriental dances." Exactly what spectators saw on the opening night and subsequent evenings is lost to history. Threats of municipal censorship and the removal—and later restoration—of announced dance numbers turned the Blüthner-Saal's recital programs into head-scratching guesswork.

The Chief of the Theatre-Division of Berlin's police department, Helmut von Glasenapp, declared Sacchetto's inclusion of the "pretty young ladies" to the dance-concert an affront to public morality. Before a special showing to the vice police on February 25th, Anita protested that she would not perform before such idiots, although postcards of her in revealing costumes and bare shoulders were already being hawked to a fascinated populace. To forestall a public ban by the Prussian constables, Rita slightly altered the program notes, adding to the confusion and salacious luster of the run.

Dance-School Rita Sacchetto provided two choreographic surprises to the Berlin aficionados of Terpsichore: a saucy 16-year-old Anita Berber and her visual inversion, the eccentric Valeska Gert, a 24-year-old Jewish dancer of the grotesque. Surviving photographic images indicate that evening included three Berber solos:

1) "Allegory of Spring"

2) "The Rose"

3) "Diana, the Huntress"

In the *tableaux vivants*, Anita appeared once again as a veiled Zephir in Friedrich Rücket's neoclassical trifle "Zephir, Amor, and Psyche," where Rita embodied the vanquished Psyche. Gert concluded the dramatic evening with a scandalous parody of "The Rose," entitled "Dance in Orange."

Anita Berber dances "Allegory of Spring," 1916

Born Gerturd Valeska Samosch into a petty Jewish merchant family in Berlin North, Valeska Gert fantasized about a career in dance her entire childhood. In 1915, already in her early twenties, Gert made the rounds at Max Reinhardt's Deutsches Theater. Arthur Kahane, the theatre's esteemed dramaturg, advised her to study at Maria Moissi's acting studio after watching the ugly duckling's amusing twists and turns. Although Gert naturally resisted Kahane's sage guidance at first, he convinced her otherwise. The rubber-faced woman's forte was clearly eccentric character—manifested through a wild and exaggerated sense of movement.

Madame Moissi herself intuited an original acting talent in Gert's characterizations. The untested comedienne showed up every day in the studio as a new and distinct stage persona: first as Goethe's Gretchen, then as Medea, then as the boy Vittorino, and finally as Amme, Juliet's wet nurse. Each of Gert's impersonations contained some essential character truth and fascinating psychic reinterpretation. Whether the improvisionally-minded Gert was up to the strict discipline of the Deutsches Theater ensemble remained questionable.

"The Rose," Atelier Alex Binder, 1916

When Rita Sacchetto auditioned Moissi's girls, Gert and her girlfriend, Brigitte Riha, were chosen along with Anita and a few more classically-toned ballerina types. Precisely how to use Gert's manic eccentricism was left to chance. Sacchetto granted her a kind of carte blanche to perform an independent solo.

According to Gert, the rehearsals and tepid costume designs of Rita's troupe bored her grievously. Each dancer, outfitted in pale shades of pastel blue or red, moved with predictable grace and faux elegance. The individual numbers systematically lacked true color or verve. The dowdy loner decided to single-handedly obliterate the sweetness and bland romanticism of the evening.

Twenty-four hours before the studio opening, Gert crafted a bizarre costume from orange silk fabric and iridescent blue ribbons. She chalked her face a deathly white and

"Diana, the Huntress"

painted yellow circles around her eyes. Supported by thin orange shoulder straps, Gert's dress ended in an above-the-knee explosive flounce, like the baggy trousers of an overgrown schoolboy. The shiny azure ribbons wrapped around her neck and ankles further mimicked a ballerina's accoutrements gone colorblind and mad. Gert's entire offbeat getup and garish makeup could be viewed not only as an aesthetic provocation, but as a mocking citation of Anita's traditional stiff pink tutu that imitated the refined texture and shape of rose petals, blossoming in the morning sun.

On stage, Gert's transgressive "Dance in Orange" proved explosive.

"Dance in Orange" begins with a wounded look of refined tenderness and soon descends into Expressionistic lunacy. Valeska Gert leaps like a runaway slave, swings her arms into pendulum-like arcs, spreads her stubby fingers à la jazz hand, and distorts her unpretty face into insolent grimaces.

Two days later, the grotesque duo of Gert and Riha appeared as a between-the-films variety act at the UT am Nollendorfplatz cinema house. Gert re-enacted her "Dance in Orange" and—with Riha—a blackface version of Claude Debussy's "Golliwog's Cakewalk." Most upsetting to the police was Gert and Riha's performance of "Pierrot and Columbine" as a lesbian duet.

Despite—or because of—the Vice Commissioner's concerns, the Blüthner-Saal concert was a *succès d'estime*. Anita's psychophysical portrayal of the mythic Diana was so widely praised that the photographic studio of Alexander Binder issued a series of postcards devoted to all of her one-woman performances.

Madame Sacchetto also realized Anita's unconventional sexual appeal and added still

This page and opposite: Valeska Gert's "Dance in Orange," Atelier Alex Binder, 1916

another Berber solo to her March program, entitled "Dante's First Sight of Beatrice." Lajos Gulascy's Symbolist portrait of *Beatrice* was well known to the Berlin art crowd, but here Anita managed to wed Renaissance and modern features into a unified and seamless role. Only a contemporary Dante and his valet were absent from the stage-picture.

⊱ FIRST AFFAIR ⊰

The week before her Blüthner-Saal debut on February 24th, Anita incautiously paraded around what remained of bohemian and cabaret Berlin. Like the rest of the girls, she was asked to drum up business for the show. Mostly, Anita called on Lucie's old acquaintances and former lovers. Among them was a singularly neurotic individual, Karl Walter, living in a downtown apartment in the Friedrichstadt. A Swiss national and 43-year-old bachelor,

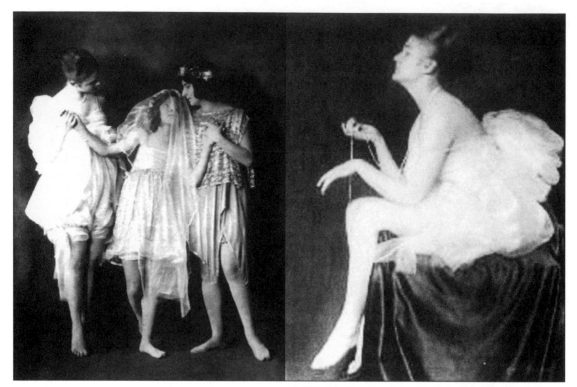

"Zephir, Amor, and Psyche," Atelier Alex Binder, 1916

Walter made his living as a crime novelist and undistinguished author of historical fantasies. He had last seen Anita after her fourteenth birthday. He barely remembered the slight, introverted child.

When Anita came knocking at his Unter den Linden door, Walter was startled. Lucie Berber's daughter had matured beyond recognition. The young dancer radiated a supreme artistic confidence and had become more beautiful than her glamorous mother. After inquiring about the health of her parents, Karl offered the girl some tea and a plate of pralines. Anita picked through the assortment of candies. Then she announced the true purpose of her surprise visit: she needed a celebrated "companion" for her premiere. The girl had come to seduce him.

Walter fidgeted at the invitation. It was an eerie and disturbing challenge more appropriate for his lust-smitten characters than its real-life neurotic creator. The big-eyed girl kicked off her shoes and waited for his response. The pudgy novelist hesitated, then leaned over to kiss her softly on the neck. Anita sprang to life. In a flash, she shed her dress and sauntered naked to his bedroom. Walter meekly followed. There the child-vixen unbuttoned the writer's jacket and shirt. She spread her china-white body over the bed and he covered it with a row of kisses. But before the unlikely Lothario sexually embraced Anita, taking the willing 16-year-old's virginity, she made him promise to bring an armful of flowers to her ballet debut. Walter agreed. The Swiss writer of historical romance fell into the ballerina's net.

On opening night, Walter, ever the gentleman, sat in the front row with a bouquet of flowers in his lap. Anita's "The Rose" jump-started the evening in grand fashion. The critics not only applauded the unknown's sparkling presentation but also marked the girl's name in the program. Anita Berber manifested both star quality and a strange, youthful authenticity.

Walter wandered backstage to Anita's dressing room, where she stood completely nude before a full-length mirror. As the excited ballerina meticulously applied makeup to her pale body, the middle-aged sycophant handed her glass after glass of champagne. Staring at her naked posterior, the transfixed Walter mumbled a long string of complimentary banalities.

Behind the stage curtain, the 17 performers dashed madly to and from their greenrooms in various states of undress. Lucie was there too, as a calming agent and inspirational aid for her daughter. Anita had not yet overcome the initial signs of extreme stage fright. When Walter caught Lucie's eye, he hesitatingly asked permission to "form a relation" with the chanteuse's daughter. Lucie laughingly replied to the shy Swiss' antiquated request. They were living in the modern age. Anita was now old enough to choose her own paramours.

Walter took home the teenage starlet after her much celebrated performance, and the pair made love for a second time.

"Korean Dance" by Atlantic Studio, 1917

❧ THE RISE TO FAME ☙

Madame Sacchetto reorganized her company in the spring of 1916. The Dance-School had achieved professional status and dropped the Berlin press clippings onto the desks of out-of-town producers to prove it. In July and August, the troupe toured Hanover, Leipzig, Frankfurt, and Hamburg. Yet even in faraway climes, Anita Berber proved to be the evening's primary draw.

Despite the teenager's uncanny ability to remember even the most insignificant details from her faded bourgeois past, the summer days and nights of 1916 all blended together into an artistic blur. Press interviews, opening-night jitters, critical acclaim, hard-bitten male admirers, extravagant hotel parties, endless arrangements in sleeping cars and train stations, and still more rehearsals all merged into a dreamy swirl. Aunt Elli Thiem acted as the family chaperone, and Walter wrote constantly. For both Anita and her audiences, however, the dance evenings provided a needed respite from news of the Kaiser's Western

Pierrotte by Atelier Alex Binder, 1917

Front campaign—a senseless morass that seemed to have stagnated into numbing trench warfare with an alarming number of casualities.

Other solo recitals followed. Anita performed at the Berlin Wintergarten in February and accompanied Sacchetto's troupe across Germany and Austro-Hungary for their summer season. *Die Dame*, a decidedly upscale women's bimonthly, featured Anita Berber as both a fashion model and fresh-faced dancer in its February and October 1917 issues.

By wintertime, Anita greatly expanded her career options: she played a minor role (as the dancing Elf) in Louis Neher's silent film *The Nixen Queen*. Like Rita, who starred in the tragic fantasy, Anita possessed both innate stage presence and hyper-expressive facial features. She was a natural asset to any motion picture director. Modeling had similar attractions as well. It paid well and involved only a fraction of the effort that concert-dancing did. In January 1918, Anita responded to an advertisement in a theatrical trade magazine. She volunteered to become a model for the Philipp Rosenthal porcelain studio.

Anita Berber's last engagement with the Sacchetto school took place at the Klindworth-Scharwenka Concert Hall in March 1918. She performed "The Rose," "Diana, the Huntress," and a *commedia dell'arte* parade "Pierrotte." After receiving a scathing review in the anarchist cultural monthly, *Kain: Zeitschrift für Menschlichkeit* (April 1918), Anita issued a personal plea to the journal's editor, Erich Mühsam. In a handwritten note, she acknowledged Mühsam's basic critique that she was too inexperienced to seamlessly fuse her spiritual essence with Expressionism's intensely individual ethos on stage—in other words, the dancer's soul-like impersonations were mostly feinted. But Berber begged Mühsam not to give up on her. Future performances would validate her theatrical authenticity and aesthetic worth.

After a year of lavish and Valentine-like reviews, German dance critics divided sharply over their assessment of Anita's performances. In *Der Künstlerische Tanz* (Leipzig: Siegels Musikalienbibliothek, 1922), Werner Suhr introduced the solo artist to his readers as one of the most unique female performers in Europe. Anita Berber was an "absolute dancer," a fresh breeze blowing across the dance floors of Berlin's staid music hall establishments. Paul Nikolaus, on the other hand, writing in *Tänzerinnen* (Munich: Delphin-Verlag, 1919), labeled Anita Berber's 1918 one-woman show as an earthbound facsimile of otherworldly Expressionism. The dancer's youthful desire and longing for adventure were sincerely enacted but ultimately incomplete and psychologically unengaging. Like her exotic, silken costumes, Anita appeared outwardly to inhabit fantastic environs, yet an essential part of her personality was scenically absent. She lacked the emotional core of a true artist. The 19-year-old could not yet draw on life-changing experiences of total fulfillment or real failure.

Anita soldiered on.

At the end of the summer in 1918, the struggling artist promised Lene Grimm-Reiter that she would perform two pieces for her Berlin dance studio's annual recital. Three days before the concert at the Blüthner-Saal, Anita canceled, claiming she was recovering from a bout of influenza. Leni Riefenstahl, a young and fresh-faced understudy, replaced the main attraction, copying each and every Berber pose. It was Leni's first performance and it successfully launched her celebrated career as an *Ausdruckstänzerin* and film actress.

Riefenstahl's memories of Anita at that time are curious and instructive. She described the starlet as "a fascinating human being with a boyish figure, she had already been very well-known thanks to the nude dances she performed on small stages and at nightclubs. Her body was so perfect that her nakedness never seemed obscene." (*Memoiren*, Munich: Knaus, 1987). Despite Riefenstahl's claim to the contrary, Berber had not yet appeared naked on any stage in 1918. The truly sexually provocative side of Anita Berber would not emerge for several seasons. The sinister eroticism that Anita projected then was hidden behind a mildly risqué theatricalism and smiling veneer.

In her first public statement, published in the trade journal *Das Organ der Variete-Welt* (October 1918), Anita defined her uncertain stage status. Despite her constant appearances in popular venues, where she competed with street jugglers and variety animal acts, the woman-of-the-hour thought of herself as a "serious artiste." Newspaper reviewers needed to critically consider her choreographic work, not the flashy environments where she performed nor the academic aesthetics of the moment.

Anita Berber's provocative gestures depict severely contrasting modes of delicacy, vivaciousness, and ease. We follow the artist's movements as she strives forward with her extraordinary emotional technique, devoted to the set rhythm. In a certain way, she seems bound to those dancers who express similar pronouncements. But Anita's search for expressive possibilities is secondary. In her dances, adventure precedes personal desire. On the dance floor, Anita reveals a longing for experience. Her dance embodies a search for wisdom. She understands the tenderness of her movements, which she submits to the rhythm of the dance, and then ecstatically descends into a slow disintegration. She presents a strange picture because of the girlish and tart uniformity of her limbs. But Anita's dance is not a pretense. We discover in it a self-conscious portrait of the artist's deep longing. She is someone who has not yet undergone true love or sacrifice, experiences that an artistic journey demands. Anita Berber's dance is not the impulse that awakens adventure, but a dream of it.

—**Paul Nikolaus, *Tänzerinnen***
(Munich: Delphin-Verlag, 1919)

⊰ RICHARD-OSWALD-FILMS ⊱

In the revolutionary year of 1918, Anita Berber discovered a new and more welcoming dramatic venue: she starred in the first of nine mass-market films directed by Richard Oswald, Vienna's most controversial and prolific filmmaker in the postwar era.

Like many Austrian artists who hoped to disguise their Hebraic origins, Richard Ornstein had dropped his family surname for one less likely to mark him as a Jew. In an ironic borrowing from Henrik Ibsen's *Ghosts*, he became Herr Direktor Oswald—named after the mad, syphilitic Norwegian stage figure. Already a celebrated performer and director in the stuffy Hapsburgian theatrical milieu, the restless innovator was also something of a technical wizard.

In 1914, Oswald, then 34, began to script and produce commercial films, each with a timely social message. He worked quickly and intuitively, frequently shooting several features simultaneously. By the early Twenties, Oswald achieved renown in Central Europe for his amazing output and singular artistry; the frenetic Wiener crafted as many as five full-length pictures per year.

Oswald's specialty was the exotic and the offbeat. He often blended genres—the psychological thriller threaded with comic interludes; the costume romance overturned by occult atmospherics; the family drama splashed with horror effects—to complicate the storytelling and to attract larger audiences. Oswald also had a showman's instinct for fresh acting talent. By 1916, he gathered enough financial backing to establish his own motion-picture company, Richard-Oswald-Filmen. The screenwriter-director-producer was clearly a Viennese original.

Just as fellow and equally ambitious Jews from the expiring Austro-Hungarian Empire went on to Berlin, Paris, London, New York, and Los Angeles to organize and promote the debased novelty, Oswald understood the motion picture's raw commercial appeal and its ineffable magic to engage and transform working-class viewers. Like his young spectators, Oswald's movie heroes and ingénues, in both comic and tragic presentations, manically sought freedom and material happiness. The influence of newspaper critics over the immediate success or popularity of his flashy movies was uncertain, sometimes even contrary. German film audiences for the most part demanded novelty, glamour, sensation, the very qualities that educated theatre and dance reviewers rotely dismissed. Oswald, like his betters, thought weightier moral issues should be consigned to intellectual journals and the national stage.

Joining a tide of young actors from Max Reinhardt's prestigious theatre companies (with soon-to-be international stars, like Conrad Veidt, Werner Krauss, and Reinhold Schünzel), Anita enjoyed the high praises of a nation hungry for indigenous screen idols and saucy beauties. Her flapper-like looks and ability to project abstract emotional states fit well into Oswald's dense narrative web. She was ideally presented as another tradition-defying rebel who fought savagely to push aside the yoke of 19th-century familial constraints.

Oswald cast Anita to play the title role in *The Story of Dida Ibsen*. The film, the company's second feature adapted from Margarete Böhme's oeuvre of popular female melodramas, was shot in Vienna in May 1918. Plotting and unusually static, it was considered an unmediated "actors' film." But Anita did not disappoint. Her wide-eyed Dida suffered all the torments appropriate to an Oswald heroine. She flees from an arranged marriage on her wedding day; becomes impregnated by a cowardly lover; opens

Anita and Werner Krauss in *The Story of Dida Ibsen*, 1918

a restaurant; marries an old, malaria-addled explorer, who turns out to be a weird sadist as well as a snake enthusiast; watches him die of his tropical maladies; returns to her despondent lover, who is also terminally ill and suicidal. Dida finally goes home and begs forgiveness from her unloving family.

One particular scene in *The Story of Dida Ibsen* upset the German censors and caused the film to be limited to adult audiences. Galen, Dida's Kaiser-like husband, decided to introduce a cobra into his sadist love-play. From a lacquered black boot, he pulls out a serpent and encourages the scaly thing to slither from his shoulder over to and around Dida's neck. Just then, the servant girl, Maria, holding a riding crop, enters the boudoir and commands the master to his knees. The old brute dutifully falls to the floor and Maria begins to lash him unceasingly. While Galen moans in sexual ecstasy, the servant girl chortles triumphantly to her mistress. The mustached beast has shockingly become the bottom in an S/M tango—a typical Oswald surprise.

Released in September, *The Story of Dida Ibsen* was held up in Berlin until the duration

The House of the Three Girls, 1918

of the war for nine weeks. The reviewer from *Lichtbildbühne* (#14, December 1918) declared the film to be "clean" and "thrilling," if understandably "sick" and "unusual" for a less enlightened public. *Der Film* (#49, December 7, 1918) also thought *Dida* to be utterly "strange" but, nonetheless, heralded the complex acting and "quality" directing. Anita's star appeared to be rising with that of her nonpareil director.

Berber's next film under Oswald's direction, *The House of the Three Girls*, did not receive such a warm embrace from the Entente's war-weary filmgoers. Based partly on Franz Schubert's light opera and partly on episodes from the Viennese composer's love life, the bio-epic was helmed two months after *Dida*. To be sure, its lush, if innocuous, nineteenth-century atmosphere found itself out of synch with the increasingly cynical populace. Anita portrayed a coquettish ballerina, who abandons a blind, old count for the charms of a raffish baron, played by Conrad Veidt. Once more, Oswald's performers were highly praised but *The House of the Three Girls* itself was derided for its cheap sentimentality and impressionistic romantic account. After the initial reviews, which panned the feature, Oswald threatened one acerbic Berlin film writer from the *Vossische Zeitung* with a defamation suit. The case was quickly and secretly settled out of court.

➣➣ "A TOTALLY PERVERTED WOMAN" ⤳⤳

Motion pictures altered Anita Berber's public persona and upended her carefully constructed sense of self. In the final months of the Kaiser's Second Reich, Anita had passed through two starkly opposed worlds of art and commerce: from the proscenium stage with its elevated notions of choreographic perfection to the hit-or-miss demimonde of the popular film. Despite her many achievements, absent still was the voice of an authentic, actualized personality.

In the fall of 1918, a balletmaster named Pirelli took charge of Anita's career. He shaped her presentational style and refocused the teenager's sex appeal. Pirelli took Anita and Aunt Elli to Prague and Vienna. And, according to Lania, it was during an after-hours party at Vienna's Hotel Bristol that the German Madonna finally metamorphosed into a depraved vixen-child, her true, chosen self.

The celebrants at the Bristol were the same mix of high society, war profiteers, haughty female aristocrats, decorated military officers, and variety entertainers that animated the Sacchetto parties during previous tours. But, now with the war slowly drawing to a disastrous conclusion for the Central Powers, the atmosphere had decidedly shifted. Fear of defeat with its unknown social consequences distorted everything. Revelers in Berlin and Vienna now eschewed international politics and battlefield talk; they obsessed over the local, the immediate, the pleasurable, which always led back to sex.

As the evening's petty flirtations turned to suggestive whispers and drunken groping,

Die Dame #10, February 1917

Anita stood up and enacted a passionate tango with Mia, an attractive strawberry-blonde and the partner of a notorious lesbian named Ellen. While the crowd gathered around the inebriated dancers, Anita methodically palmed the girl's nipples until the giddy blonde nearly collapsed in orgasmic surrender. Ellen rushed to support her unsteady lover and commanded Anita to sit down. The air crackled with tension and sexual provocation.

Flushed with French brandy, an Austrian banker grabbed Anita's stocking-clad calf and attempted to kiss her ankle. The porcelain-skinned teen shoved him off the sofa to make room for Mia.

On the other side of the room, a cavalry officer plunged his hand down the open blouse of a tousle-haired housewife and felt her breasts. The banker's wife, Dolli Mainz, shook with laughter and coyly hoisted up the hem of her skirt in order to let the soldier marvel at her legs. Ellen pleaded for a bit of decorum. But Anita took stage center again when she stood and lifted her evening dress over her hips.

The partygoers applauded Anita's daring and the banker demanded a contest for the most beautiful female gams. Anita yanked a hair-clasp from Mia's head and, after the drunken girl's hair fell down to her shoulders, planted a hard kiss on the blonde's mouth. Once it was clear that Ellen had enough of the ballerina's antics and decided to rescue the situation, Anita leaped at her nemesis, pawing at Ellen's face and scratching her hand.

Someone separated the two and Anita shouted that she wanted to dance. The banker concurred but the dance had to be done in the nude. The crowd chanted, "Naked, naked."

Anita calmly stepped out of her dress and started to spin in mad desperation. Her nude body now a weapon, the dancer taunted the crowd, who suddenly stepped back in palpable fright. Anita Berber danced naked for the first time.

Afterward the 19-year-old retreated to the bathroom. She felt sick and nauseated. Staring at the mirror, she penciled two enormous eyebrows on her forehead, blotted green shadow around her eyes, and painted her lips an unnatural greasy crimson. It was a bizarre mask that Anita would never completely remove.

The startled crowd gossiped nonstop about the shameless showgirl. Who was she and where had she come from? Dolli remarked grimly that Anita was a "totally perverted woman." In a few months, the world would learn the truth of Dolli's prophetic characterization.

⋙ A NEW WORLD ⋘

During her Budapest engagement at the Orpheum, Anita struck up a romantic affair with an AWOL Austro-Hungarian officer, Hans Neumann. He had little to offer her, except kind words and male companionship. After two weeks, Anita broke off all contact with the dashing lieutenant and his desperate entreaties. Their tête-à-tête meetings in cheap hotel rooms and on park benches pulled the dancer down into a deep depression. She needed to be totally free from all such bourgeois attachments. It was to be Anita's last normal heterosexual relationship.

On November 3rd, 1918, an Armistice to the Great War was declared. Budapest, the capital of the newly independent Hungary, erupted in anarchy and revolutionary violence. Anita watched from her hotel window as looters from the Hungarian lowlands and nationalist militia units torched the final markings of German-speaking rule. Anita left for Berlin.

In the cramped Budapest-Vienna train car, Anita sat shoulder-to-shoulder with Gerda, the wife of a career Austrian officer and their 12-year-old daughter Elsie. The 48-year-old paterfamilias, Oberlieutentant Josef, had lost everything in the formal surrender: his rank, vocation, and status. People like him were now extraneous, minions of an eviscerated monarchy. Anita was at least a youthful divertissement for his spouse and child. (Little did the military man know that the 19-year-old dancer would soon become his replacement and the sexual obsession of his affection-starved wife and daughter.)

Back in her mother's five-room Berlin apartment on 13 Zähringer Strasse, Anita settled in with her mother; grandmother; Aunt Elli; the Viennese conferencier, Fritz Grünbaum, and his new bride, Elisabeth Herzl.

Die Dame #5, December 1918

Die Dame published a photograph of the glamorous starlet at home in its December edition. Waldemar Titzanthal captured Anita in a rakish pose, leaning against Lucie's fireplace. The fashion-plate vixen projected two unsettling and prescient attitudes: chic confidence in her physical appearance and a forlorn acknowledgement of her fate as a dancer. Staring across the room, it seemed that Anita was contemplating a new path to achieve international attention and artistic notoriety.

CHAPTER TWO
DANCE IN THE NEW NINEVEH
(1919–1928)

Things are perhaps a little madder than usual these days. At places like the so-called Intimate Theater, there are one-acters, like "The Lesbian Lovers." I must refrain from mentioning anything more than the title. Performed by the most middling of actors and the most charmless of actresses. During the intermission there is the "Oriental Dance"—according to the placard. In reality a so-called dancer, thin as a rail, shows all of her ribs during the usual *pointe*-segment. The dance is entitled, "Morphine," and is by Mischa Spoliansky, from Poland or Bessarabia. Real morphine deadens pain but this dance causes it. I can't bear to see so many ribs. After the dance another one-acter: "Everyone Gets Half." This time there are two beds on the stage, each one in a hotel room. A hooker and two hotel guests are the actors, if you can call them that. That's how Berlin rings in the New Year.

—Rumpelstilzchen, *Täglichen Rundschau* (January 4, 1923)

Anita Berber's dance repertoire, to be sure, bestowed the Berlin audiences with all the requisite exotica that the wartime censors would allow and then some. But the shameless Madonna had yet to publicly display her naked body. Anita's performances were still masked in silken costumes, erotically internalized, practically oblique. Her pre-1919 movement studies were still informed by Dalcroze's *Eurhythmics* and Sacchetto's *poses plastiques*. Nude dancing had a different tradition.

Before the establishment of the Weimar Republic, exposed female flesh made its showy appearance in German dance halls as high art or as music hall whimsy. After 1919, everything changed.

Exactly why Berlin became the world showcase of nude dance and the erotic revue-sketch is commonly explained by social historians as a direct consequence of Weimar's Great Inflation. Naked Dance was just another by-product that exemplified the city's unbroken moral degeneration. Yet mass poverty, and sexual promiscuity that accompanied the devaluation of the mark, was only one factor. Women and teenage girls had already paraded their naked torsos onstage more than a decade earlier when the German metropolis was quite prosperous and Wilhelmian Vice Commissioners acted with civic impunity.

Berlin's brand of Naked Dance had its roots in the late nineteenth-century Germanic revolt against all things rigidly bourgeois and hypocritically Christian. It began with the collapse of Lutheranism as a national communal belief and social control. And it seeped into the writings of Friedrich Nietzsche.

⚓ THE DANCING PHILOSOPHERS ⚓

For Nietzsche, "joyous dance" and the "body's wisdom" were prerequisites for truth and self-knowledge. In *The Birth of Tragedy* (1872), *The Gay Science* (1882), and *Thus Spake Zarathustra* (1885), the reclusive philosopher championed the pre-Christian ethos

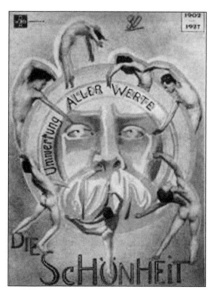

Die Schönheit **cover, December 1927**

of vitalistic spontaneity and muscular hedonism. "Any day that precluded dance," the sickly Nietzsche wrote, "was a day lost." What was unclear in this transformative and existential philosophy was the precise meaning of the word *dance*: was it being used metaphorically for the Hellenistic virtues that embraced flesh and spirit equally, or did it refer to the actual motions of the human body that channeled—or resulted from—a surfeit of life-giving energy?

In 1902, the San Francisco-born Isadora Duncan came to Berlin, and for two hours demonstrated a shocking new dance form. What she depicted seemed totally unrelated to

French ballet, interpretive folk dance, or contemporary social dance. Copying images from classical Greek urns or Renaissance paintings, Isadora crawled, leaped, pranced, and glided across the Kroll-Oper stage while the orchestra played Chopin, Liszt, and Brahms. Instead of tights, padded skirts, or a tutu, the American radical wore loose, diaphanous garments that graphically revealed her limbs and free-flowing movements. More startling, like her Greek predecessors, she danced barefoot. To the Berlin critics, Isadora looked practically naked.

The New World provocateur claimed that she merely following Nietzsche's edicts. Her choreography, inspired by ancient, non-Christian values, was in fact modern, an analog to Naturalist acting, a scenic reaction against current dance traditions that, according to the California dance-philosopher, were ossified and without real content. Isadora's movements and costume displayed the primal rhythms of the liberated body.

More than anything, Isadora's fresh attitude and sleek feminine beauty won over the Berlin skeptics. In their considered judgments, transgressive innovation was now wedded to cultural ideas and social reform. A full-scale revolution in German choreography had finally been launched.

MAGDELEINE G.,
◆ THE HAUSFRAU SOMNAMBULIST ◆

When Magdeleine G., the hypnotic (or dream) dancer, first appeared on a Munich cabaret stage in the spring of 1904, her audiences mainly came to gawk at the medical curiosity. Could hypnotic suggestion from the Swiss doctor Emile Magnin with the addition of classical music transmute a rather ordinary Hausfrau into some kind of wild dervish dancer? A host of local physicians declared Magdeleine's altered consciousness as bona fide possession and several—like the steely investigator of occult phenomena Dr. Albert von Schrenck-Notzing—even published treatises on it. Typical was a report

Magdeleine Comforts an Imaginary Child in Emile Magnin, **L'Art et l'Hypnose, 1905**

from a Dr. L. Self in the *Münchner Neueste Nachrichten* (March 16, 1904): "Magdeleine appears quiet and skillful. From the moment, however, that, through Magnin's fixed gaze and gestures, she is put into her strange state, a complete change takes place. Her features becomes rigid, a squint is in her eye. [...] Suddenly, with the coming of music, a new and striking change occurs in Magdeleine's whole appearance. The features become lively. Magdeleine rises and accompanies the music and shouted suggestions with gestures and pantomimic expressions revealing sadness, bliss, rapture, rage—i.e., all the emotions—in a rather precise way, even according to pitch, volume, sound color, intervals, and rhythms. If the music is suddenly interrupted, catalepsis follows."

It was Magdeleine's absolute and startling corporal transformations that brought her to the attention of German dancers and critics. At the sound of a chord on the piano or a shouted suggestion, Magdeleine magically changed from one emotional state to another.

Olga Desmond and Adolf Salge, 1909

Starting from a rigid catalepsy and fixed gaze, Magdeleine, under the command of her hypnotist, revealed the intriguing and rapturous worlds of her soul, moving from bliss to sadness to rage to hysteria Then, with the clap of the hands or any musical interruption, she immediately froze in position, returning her to a lifeless state. Magdeleine's spiritual intensity and expressiveness, although presented as a vaudeville novelty, further stimulated the thinking of German choreographers and movement specialists.

BERLIN'S "LIVING STATUES" AND "BEAUTY-EVENINGS"

In 1908, Wilhelmian stage decorum was shaken again by Olga Desmond's "Beauty Evenings." Appearing virtually naked at the Neuen Schauspielhaus before some 1,400

Berliners, the British-born Desmond, with her partner the athlete Adolf Salge, offered up a sensation both philosophical and erotic. If painters and sculptors are permitted the professional right to view and sketch undressed models, why should consumers of art and others be denied the same aesthetic and visual liberty? And why was the second-hand representation of the naked body acceptable but its living source forbidden?

A serious choreographer and writer as well as creator of her own dance-notation system, Desmond displayed her naked body as a "Living Statue" with such milky refinement and scenic perfection that a new generation of German critics were immediately taken with the novelty. Henry de Ury had already mounted "Living Statue" sensations at the Wintergarten variety house in 1900. But de Ury's marble-looking friezes displayed military engagements, biblical scenes, and patriotic celebrations. What flesh his still-life performers revealed veered toward historical and character narrative.

"The Venus of London" stressed the harmonious shape of the female body rather than just form in movement or the placement of symbolic types. Sexy *tableaux vivants* and Oriental harem dances formed the basis of Desmond's stage work. Any application of jewelry or clothing, any superficial beautification was mostly shunned. Unlike Isadora or Magdeleine, this performer could not be said to dance with prurient or occult intent. Olga and Adolf remained still.

Even if she did not always satisfy the reviewers' artistic expectations, Desmond proclaimed undeniable idealistic values and was the tangible realization of a chaste and refined notion of impeccable feminine form. Raw, unvarnished beauty rather than nudity was emphasized in the Desmond-Salge stage pictures.

Threats of government prosecution over obscenity and nudity in 1909, however, caused Desmond to abandon public dance for the photography studio and publishing.

THE *NACHTLOKAL* AND ❧ AMATEUR PERFORMANCE ❧

In the months preceding the 1918 Armistice, a crude subset of Naked Dance surfaced in Berlin's corner bars and thirty-eight registered cabarets and nightclubs. Wartime interest in nudist health culture, Psychoanalysis, and *Ausdruckstanz* provided an intellectual facade to these smutty stripped-down shows. For the most part, the *Tingel-Tangel* Girls did not perform completely disrobed, but wore small jewel-like coverings and silk scarves. Even with veiled breasts and genitals, war-weary spectators saw them as anatomically nude.

After the Kaiser's abdication, public fascination with the Naked Dance quickly increased. There was a surfeit of willing participants and private nightspots to accommodate them. Labeled *Nachtlokals*, these makeshift and illicit establishments brought nude amateur dancers and free-spending spectators into giggly, warm contact. Fifty-minute "Beauty Nights" were offered here without lectures or philosophical charade. One could even purchase companionship or outright sexual frisson with one or more of the panting artistes.

Naked Dance by Max Beckmann, 1922

35

Celly de Rheidt's "Opium," 1920

❧ CELLY DE RHEIDT ❧

Celly de Rheidt (or Celly de Rheydt, Cäcilie Schmidt, Cäcilie Funk) was one of the first dance personalities associated with the erotic postwar culture of Berlin. Her naked Ballet Troupe first performed in the fall of 1919 at the Babijou Bar and guest-starred at various Friedrichstadt cabaret venues like Siegbert Wrechinski's Schwatzer Kater and Nelson's Künstlerspiele during the next three years. For one season in 1920, Celly ran her own private theatre club in a Motzstrasse dive.

The Celly Girls themselves were quite young—between 14 and 20—and never numbered more than five. Typically, Celly's husband Lieutenant Alfred Seveloh (or Harry de Rheidt) would introduce the evenings and compare the Troupe's efforts to Isadora Duncan's free-style dances or more noble visions of the naked female body in kinesthetic movement. His pre-show blandishments grew shorter and shorter by the season.

Richard Oswald filmed the de Rheidt Ballet in October 1919. For a different novelty approach, Seveloh used Oswald's silent clips to welcome and bestill his audiences. At the beginning of February 1920, the Celly de Rheidt Ballet Troupe performed at the Villa Borngräber, the home of *Reigen's* flamboyant publisher. Wilhelm Borngräber cautioned his

The Magic of Spring, by Josef Fenneker, 1920, and Celly de Rheidt Ballet's *Czardas*, 1920

readers not to view the *Beauty Dances of Nimbus* as pornographic or risqué. That would be a sign of Wilhelmian prudery or false sophistication. Celly's work was wondrous, liberating, natural, and venerable. Her dancers were scenic emblems of a new age.

Celly de Rheidt's Ballet Troupe was forced to disband shortly after New Year's 1922 when Seveloh was charged with tax evasion. The dashing *bon vivant* claimed that Celly's luxurious lifestyle precluded any declared profit. The Naked Ballet was a money-losing operation. Despite his long and impassioned defense, the accused racketeer was sentenced to reimburse 5,400 marks to the city. Seveloh stalled paying the unprecedented fine until the summer when the inflationary mark fell to a laughable medium of exchange.

Meanwhile Celly filed for divorce and took her Troupe to Leipzig, where they performed a Grand-Guignolesque lesbian *Vampire Dance*. The critics found this emotionally darker theme more attuned to the times. In 1924, Celly married a Viennese theatre producer and settled down in Austria to be an upstanding Hausfrau, never to be heard from again. Her name as the prime choreographer of naked beauty and the Girls themselves, however, remained in constant circulation within Berlin's underworld scene.

Big-City Show by Heinz von Perckhammer

⚘ INFLATION AND COLLAPSE ⚘

The hyperinflation that brought the postwar German economy to a ruinous halt unfolded in explosive fits and starts. Every few months beginning in 1921, the Allies demanded additional payments from the Weimar government in the form of coal, iron, quality industrial goods and gold bullion. The draconian calculations from British and French auditors left little of worth in the dwindling German federal treasury. The purchasing power of German citizens would be soon ground down to almost nothing. (A single British cigarette in 1923 had the exact value in marks that a luxury grand piano, fresh from the Steinway factory, commanded two short years before.)

Practically every hard good item that could be placed in a container trunk was shipped out of Germany by greedy tradesmen and entrepreneurs, who roamed the countryside in search of prewar artifacts and cherished heirlooms. Overnight, it seemed that the nation had just one desirable commodity that could not be easily exported: sex. Germany still possessed indescribable erotic possibilities for pocket change.

For tourists from Dollarika (the U.S.), Guilderland (Holland), and Yeniwara (Japan) especially, the entire city of Berlin had transformed into a penny candy store-*cum*-brothel. A few dollars, guilders, francs, lira, or a handful of yen bought weeks of loving embraces and perverse affection from virginal Mädchen, silk-stockinged Fräuleins, 10-year-old Doll-Boys, and hefty General's wives. A foreigner could choose from any combination of willing participants for any kind of orgiastic *Bummel*. The sextropolis was awash in cocaine and opium (rolled into those British cigarettes) as well. Otherwise penny-pinching Ausländer could—and did—live it up like lust-smitten potentates or high-stepping maharajahs.

Slave Dance by Heinz von Perckhammer

In January 1921, a dollar bill officially traded for seven precious German marks; nine months later, its value increased tenfold. By the summer of 1922, the same greenback was happily exchanged for 7,500 marks, or 20 hand-tailored silk nightgowns. A "50 Groschen Bread," the mainstay of working families, was going for 30 times its namesake and then could only be acquired from American Quaker or Salvation Army soup-kitchen vans that roamed Germany's slum districts and its depressed suburbs.

At the end of September 1923, the U.S. dollar equaled one billion free-falling marks. And the mark still tumbled by the day, by the hour. In city marketplaces, cabbage heads cost 50 million per; nicotine-addled factory-workers dried, shredded, and then rolled the inedible outer leaves into puffable ersatz cigars. The October 1923 issue of *Der Junggeselle* (#41), which included a photograph of Anita Berber's "Pritzel-Figurine" dance, was considered a bargain at 550 million marks. In three weeks, the dollar, if it could be found, sold for 6.6 billion marks in the Friedrichstadt.

On November 20, 1923, a new German currency, the Rentenmark, was announced. This unit of money was backed by actual gold reserves and immediately stanched the staggering financial and social bloodletting. After two years of constant economic instability, the Weimar government discovered a means to satisfy both its international creditors and frightened, malnourished populace.

The Republic remarkably survived the Great Inflation.

MORE DISTURBING THAN NUDE

Dance-Evening Valeska Gert by Koser,
Ulk, November 12, 1926

Historically, the work of Valeska Gert defies standard definition. Critics of her early performances in 1917 refused to accept her presentations as dance or theatre. Her eccentric style of movement and bizarre characterizations were just too ugly, disjointed and, worst of all, short—with some improvised pieces lasting less than a minute. One enraged spectator declared that Gert wasn't even human: she was a wild beast chewing up the stage. In the end, Gert billed herself as a "Grotesque Dancer."

A favorite of the international avant-garde, Gert appeared in milestone productions created by the Dadas and Expressionists. Bertolt Brecht declared her to be the truest "Epic Actor" alive. Jean Cocteau saw her as

Surrealism personified. Soviet biographers suggested that Gert was Sergei Eisenstein's only real female love interest.

In fact, Gert pioneered the genre that we call Performance Art. Her material appeared to follow no fixed pattern, never dumbly repeated, only a repertory of sordid caricatures, weird moods, and darkly satiric atmospheres. A typical Gert evening would consist of "sound studies" of crying babies, a stylized striptease, a young samurai's enactment of suicide, the manic flow of traffic on the Berlin Kudamm, the unfolding of a French prostitute's day as she slowly acknowledges her hopeless condition, an attack on classical ballet, and a boxing match.

In appearance, Gert was the counter-Berber. Yet her ultimate goal had many similarities to that of the Dresden Madonna: both wanted to annihilate traditional dance's treacly forms and its synthetic meanings.

❧ NAKED REVUE ❧

The Naked Dance in the early years of the Weimar Republic needed to be cloaked in various cultural disguises. The not-quite-legal productions could either be presented as exercises in pure Naturalism, high art, or avant-garde novelty. Studious lectures, ornamental theatrical backdrops, and accompaniments of classical or modern music were typical strategies to hide the prurient enterprise. There was stripping on the Berlin stage but the teasing had to be framed with a faux intellectual cover. By the end of the Inflation period, audiences tired of the subterfuge.

A new use for nude performers was created in the Naked Revue. The Girls teams were a splashy visual element, if an essential one, in mammoth evenings of character-driven plot, popular music, comic bits, and snappy dialogue. Once again, nude female bodies paraded themselves before delighted Berliner eyes, yet their look and meaning had changed markedly. These naked dancers no longer embodied languorous visions from

James-Klein Ballet *Brandenburg Gate,* **1919**

classical antiquity but high-stepping erotic symbols of the future; the top-hatted and silk-clad Girls were smiling robotrons, marching and twirling to the sounds of the shimmy and Charleston.

The modern revue was conceived in Paris and New York during the decade before the Great War. It was a colorful expansion of familiar variety formats, seasoned with music hall frivolity and stylish Art Deco imagery. Naked dancers were officially billed as artistes and, above his Broadway marquees, Flo Ziegfeld advertised the annual productions as "Follies." Atmospherically the French and American nude routines were light and sophisticated. When the New York Vice Police attempted to shut down Ziegfeld's production for public obscenity, the 1922 *Follies'* playbills overnight included small pencils and blank sheets. Spectators were encouraged to view the naked Ziegfeld models like professional sketch-artists in a studio setting. Ziegfeld's lawyers, borrowing from Olga Desmond's playbook, argued successfully that the Follies' audiences had the same rights to mark the shapes of unfrocked women as their Greenwich Village counterparts.

In Berlin, the Naked Revue took a different turn. It drew from the indigenous erotic

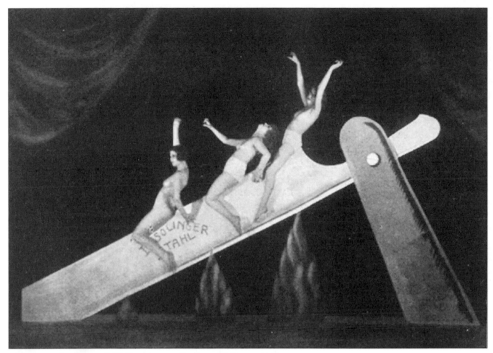

"Slide on the Razor," Haller Revue *Under and Over*, 1923

cabaret and *Tingel Tangel*. The *berlinsch* conferencier had a much larger role, usually as the starring attraction, and the nude features here were considerably less coy. In 1923, three major revues opened at large theatre or variety houses: *The World Unveiled* (at the James-Klein-Revue), *For Everyone!* (Charell Revue) and *Under and Over* (Haller Revue).

Klein's productions were considered the most garish, the most smutty, with endless numbers of bare-breasted South Sea islanders or high-heeled Fräuleins in upturned skirts. Each season at the Komische Oper proved more startling than the last. The program titles themselves indicated the degree of sensationalism: *What the World Has Not Seen* (1924), *From A To Z* (1925), *Berlin Without a Blouse* (1926), *The Sins of the World* (1927), *Strictly Prohibited!* (1927), *The World Applauds* (1927), *Everyone Naked!* (1927), *Take It Off!* (1928), *Goddamnit—1000 Women!* (1928, remounted a few weeks later as the slightly trimmed-down *1000 Naked Women!*), *Houses of Love* (1928), *The Paradise of Sweet Women* (1930), and *From Bed to Bed* (1930).

A modern dancer and Max Reinhardt actor, Erik Charell placed a greater premium on

Scenes from Cabaret Revue: *Creation* **and** *First Sin*, 1928

fantastic visual and music effects. To a large degree, the Charell-Revue worked from an international menu with individual numbers dropped in from London, Paris, and New York. The British choreographer John Tiller was responsible for the mechanical displays of the Tiller-Girls. The erotic Corps de Ballet was usually imported from Paris. Eccentric novelty dances originated from the American vaudeville circuit. Only the humor and cabaret solos were authentically German.

An opera enthusiast, Herman Haller emphasized a more thorough integration of music, dance, and parody sketch. Lawrence-Tiller-Girl drills—"often copied but never surpassed"—brushed up against his Haller-Girl naked kick-lines. Blackout sex farces were followed by torch-singing chanteuses. A typical evening would consist of 50 short acts, all held together by a single erotic theme. More than anyone, Haller resembled Ziegfeld with his tony casts and suave persona.

The Golden Age of the Berlin Revues ended around 1928. They had become too expensive, too lavish, and no longer fit the mood of the time. Musical films were more efficient in telling dramatic love stories and providing cosmopolitan fizzle. The old intimate eroticism of Naked Dance could be better viewed in nightclubs and on the cabaret stage. There the Girls were once again within arm's reach and the saucy routines short, striking, and unpredictable.

CHAPTER THREE
BERLIN'S NAKED GODDESS

(1919–1922)

I saw her [Anita Berber] once at a party in the house of a famous art dealer. She arrived in a magnificent fur coat and violet silk shoes. Whenever she opened her fur cloak her naked body was disclosed. She did it with a gesture of dignified naturalness, as though her strange costume were the accepted fashion of the day. Life in Berlin had hardened people to such an extent that nothing seemed to shock them.

—Rom Landau, *Seven* (London: Nicholson & Watson, 1936)

For urban-dwellers of the defeated Entente nations, the Allied victory inaugurated a period of social uncertainty and dread. The Central Powers' regal leaders, vast national boundaries, old currencies, and aristocratic social structures vanished or were tossed aside. And into this unprecedented political free-for-all came anarchy and civil insurrection. Both left-wing radicals and reactionary nationalists established zones or enclaves, where workers' councils or self-proclaimed militia leaders struggled to apply new rules of law. All of Germany and Austria, pundits predicted, could either go the way of Leninist Russia or Pilsudski's Poland.

In January 1919, a modicum of stability arrived when pro-Bolshevik insurgents were pushed off the main streets of Berlin and their organizers summarily executed. In faraway Weimar, a constitutional republic led by the Socialists was about to be declared.

The erasure of the German and Austrian monarchies from the European governing rostrums

Eberhard von Nathusius

transformed the cultural climate of the vanquished nations overnight. No one really knew who had the right or power to establish proper civil behavior, delimit offensive aesthetic boundaries, and even what or how to censor previously forbidden activities. In a matter of weeks, German-speaking graphic artists, theatre practitioners, filmmakers, and writers had invented new formulas, manufactured new vehicles, and sought out new avatars to fuel and people their erotic dreamscapes.

In the midst of this seemingly endless chaos, Eberhard von Nathusius, a young screenwriter from Star-Film Productions, discovered Anita Berber.

A stock player in Richard Oswald's Vienna-Berlin film stable, Anita satisfied von Nathusius' deepest personal longings and writerly needs. Like the tragic silent-film diva, Gilda Langer, Eberhard's previous Pygmalion, Anita always performed some version of herself. When everything in art seemed impermanent or ersatz, she was naturally stylish, serious but charming, self-involved and breathtakingly authentic.

For Anita, von Nathusius' romantic attentions were a welcome diversion from pressing family matters. Fritz Grünbaum concocted plans for the outgoing Lucie as a star chanteuse in Rudolf Nelson's Berlin cabaret stage, but had none for her red-haired daughter. Just then it seemed there were few career venues for the 19-year-old dancer. Eberhard was at least debonair and possessed a considerable hard-currency fortune. Mostly he provided a means of independence, a way of leaving home. They married during the bloody month of January 1919.

"Valse Impromptu," Atelier Eberth, 1919 and Otto Goetze, 1924

✺ HELIOBABAL'S KISS ✺

On January 23rd and 29th, Anita performed her first evening-length one-woman show at the Blüthner-Saal. Superficially, it was an evening with many of the antiquated trappings of prewar culture. At the piano, Edgar Cleve played Romantic interludes by Frédéric Chopin, his adaptation of Richard Wagner's *Die Walküre*, Johannes Brahms, and Franz Liszt as well an original "Waltz Caprice."

Elegant postcards of each dance, captured in Anny Eberth's and Dora Kallmus-Arthur Benda's Berlin photographic studios, were sold in the foyer.

Anita's first-act presentation consisted of a series of four short dances:

1) "Valse Impromptu": This is a solo waltz by Liszt, executed in a green dress, cut to look like rows of leaves, with a flowing white, silkened train. (A more daring drawing from 1924 revealed a single breast down to the nipple.)

"Pritzel Figurine," Atelier Eberth, 1919

2) "Pritzel Figurine": Dressed as an Indian court dancer, Anita creates a playful variation on the "Nutcracker Suite" ballet. In Anita's rendition, one of Lotte Pritzel's ceramic figures suddenly comes alive to the faux-Romantic music of Anton Rubinstein. After the Figurine awakens and twirls across the stage, the straps of her dress fall down her arms. She looks up and laughs.

3) "Golliwog's Cakewalk": The light-hearted number is yet another variation on the Debussy ragtime favorite. Golliwog (Anita), the popular doll character with a fixed smile, leans back, high-kicks, and struts its way around the stage.

4) "La Masque": Anita wears a carnivalesque silver facemask pulled high over a Hussar-like fur hat. (The stunning headpiece itself, created in the Atelier Plotow and Schädler, will make fashion news.) It is unclear whether Anita's mysterious creature is intended to be a woman in Fasching drag or a depraved male warrior, undergoing a rite of passage. While

"Golliwog's Cake Walk," Atelier D'Ora, 1922

"La Masque," Atelier Eberth, 1919 and Becker & Maar, 1919

Cleve plays a lurid "pas de fleurs" from Léo Delibes' *Coppélia*, a signature ballet piece from the Anna Pavlova repertoire, a red-trousered Anita enacts the role of a polymorphous Pan, leaping effortlessly and waving a rose-vine scepter before make-believe partygoers.

The second part of the evening began on a more traditional note.

5) "Czardas": This Hungarian rite-of-spring village initiation is executed to the rich orchestrations of Ludwik Grossmann's interpretative folk melodies.

6) "Heliogabal": A pantomimic glorification of the decadent Roman emperor in ancient Syria—a subject of two popular German novels—is enacted with perverse ambiguity. (A historical figure whose sexual dysphoria culminated in a bizarre cultish ceremony, Heliogabal reportedly forced his supplicants to worship him as both a sacred temple

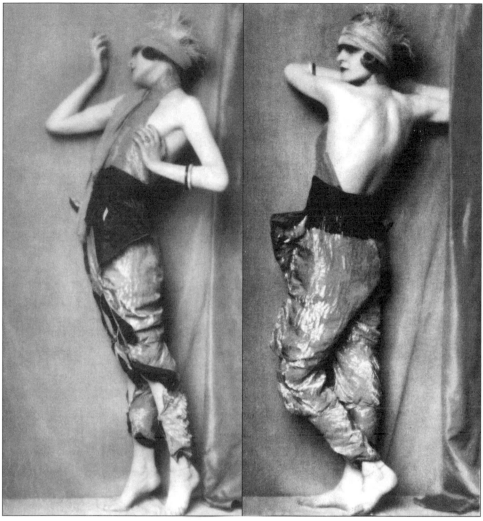

"Heliogabal," Atelier D'Ora, 1922

prostitute and the reincarnation of the deadly Sun Goddess.) Camille Saint-Saëns' *Danse macabre* provides the rhythmic inspiration for Anita's vision of demonic sacrifice and ecstatic defilement.

7) "Valse Triste": This is a flirtatious, contemporary fan dance to the music of the Finnish composer, Jean Sibelius.

8) "Caprice Espagnol": In a thoroughly transgressive finale, Anita plays a character of indeterminate gender. Here the confident provocateuress, in a stylish gold-and-black wardrobe, prances about as a "Spanish Dandy." Moritz Moszkowski's *Bullfight Sonate*

"Valse Triste," Atelier D'Ora, 1922

underscores the overt meaning of the audacious conclusion. It was as if Anita Berber, a double-sexed matador from some hypereroticized future, has accepted Berlin's challenge to a life-and-death struggle. The Dandy is triumphant.

"Caprice Espagnol," Atelier D'Ora, 1922

The January performances had formerly established Anita as a "New Wonder in the Art of Dance" as a performance critic in the *Elegante Welt* declared in its Spring issue.

> During grey antiquity, the Sungod danced in front of the enthusiastic crowd who thought that they were experiencing God. They believed that all earthly delight was in Heliobabal's kiss.
>
> "Roaring music made all of the audience's screaming disappear who—in their crazy longing—pushed further and further towards the front, who murdered, stamped to death and strangled—in order to get closer to this kiss, in order to become part of it, to be the giving one. The Sungod gets up, raises his hands. He spins around like a turning circle, he is dancing. One stamps, one murders—in order to see this death. Dying people lay in the aisles; pillars are splashed with blood. Pieces of torn clothes, worn-out shoes— Heliogabal is dancing...."
>
> And Anita Berber brings this dance to life—with sweet, intoxicating sensuality that is enriched by Couperas' words. Miraculous, all covered in gold, her metallic body lures the sun while two Moorish boys effectively manipulate the backdrops.
>
> —**"Anita's Berber's 'Heliogabal'"**
> (Elegante Welt #2, End of January 1919)

⚘ EROTIC FILM DIVA ⚘

In the spring of 1919, three of Richard Oswald's photoplays, with Anita in supporting parts, were released in Germany's newest cinema palaces.

On March 20th, Richard Oswald's *Around the World in 80 Days* opened at Berlin's Marmorhaus. Adapted from the Jules Verne classic as a comic adventure and ironic travelogue, Anita played Aouda, the East Indian princess who was about to be burned next to her husband's corpse in a *sati*, the outlawed Hindu funerary ceremony. Unlike the prewar French film adaptation, Oswald emphasized the novel's grotesque and exotic thrills. Anita was already well enough recognized as a film star that the *12-Uhr-Blatt* in its review maintained that she needed no introduction or "explanation" to the filmgoing public. The girl was a costumed minx.

Around the World in 80 Days poster, 1919

Oswald's second 1919 feature, *Prostitution*, opened in Berlin two months later. The Marmorhaus called it "a Social-Hygiene Film" in garish, Expressionistic window-display posters. Unlike *Around the World*, this erotic melodrama was rushed to small film halls in underclass and proletarian neighborhoods under the title *In the Gutter of the*

Prostitution poster by Joachim Rágóczy, 1919

Big City before vice police and newspaper reviewers could rule on its salacious theme.

Kurt Tucholsky, writing in the *Berliner Volkszeitung* (May 7, 1919), praised Anita's performance as Lona, a bourgeois daughter lured into the white slave trade, and the other actors' work, but condemned the movie itself as a prime example of "Kinokitsch." For the *berlinsch* journalist, the film was a sham vehicle for "Sexual Enlightenment." Despite the imprimatur of Dr. Magnus Hirschfeld, Europe's leading authority on sexology, and its high-minded claims, Tucholsky felt Oswald's cinematic morality tale itself was a new sin: "prostitution with an aesthetic mask." After state censors deleted key scenes and the motion picture was formally banned in a number of German towns in 1921, *Prostitution* (forcibly renamed by the Prussia's Vice Commissioner as *The Yellow House*) disappeared from the Richard-Oswald-Film catalog. It joined a host of lost artifacts in the ever-deepening trunk of discarded Weimar erotica.

Different From the Others, 1919. Anita is on the far right.

Oswald's follow-up "Social-Hygienic" project, *Different From the Others*, premiered at Berlin's Apollo-Theater on May 28th. This venture proved even more problematic than *Prostitution*. Here the subterranean world of homosexual love, the Prussian code that outlawed it (Paragraph 175), its shame, and tragic consequences were frankly and provocatively addressed. Oswald had again challenged the authority of motion-picture censorship by tying it to Hirschfeld's scientific theories about the immutability of sexual desire and modern notions of "sexual intermediaries."

Anita played a minor love interest, something of a walk-on, the sister-in-law and admirer of the disgraced gay violinist, Paul Körtner. After reporting the guilt-ridden history of the blackmail payments to the authorities, Körtner (enacted by Veidt) is imprisoned for his past indiscretions with a male student. Ironically he is incarcerated with his nemesis. The violinist later commits suicide when he realizes that the public charge will also mean the end of his formally illustrious career. Hirschfeld appeared in the film's afterword, where he famously called for the repeal of Paragraph 175.

Forty individual prints of *Different From the Others* circulated across Germany during the summer of 1919. It was the centerpiece of Oswald's cunning strategy to assure the film's physical survival despite right-wing attempts to ban it. While championing its humane social message, newspaper reviews were generally mixed about *Different From the Others'* overtly tenacious tone. Although the story was based on a true incident, most journalists reacted to the "enlightened" feature as they had to Oswald's earlier work: to be sure, it dealt with a serious topic but in an emotionally hokey and melodramatic manner. After 16 months, the state ruled on *Different From the Others'* public status. It was fit for only for the consumption of the professional elite, to be seen by certified physicians and court-appointed lawyers.

❧ NEW SCANDAL ❧

According to Lania, Anita missed all of the gala spring openings in Berlin and the contentious national debates that erupted from Oswald's incendiary meditations on German life and its corrupting secrets. The renegade film starlet had returned to Vienna in April to be with Gerda and Elsie, her newest family. The decadent world there, to be sure, had none of the restrictions or predictability of an Oswald narrative.

During the week of the April 17th, the Hapsburgian capital had collapsed into civil war and internecine madness. The threesome encamped in Anita's old haunt, the Hotel Bristol in the city's neoclassical center. While the women marveled at the insurrection in the streets below on the Ringstrasse, Gerda's husband attempted to regain his position in various ministries of the rump Republic. He journeyed to a dozen small Austrian cities and villages, believing old army buddies in their hometowns would take pity on him and provide suitable employment.

Meanwhile Anita took charge of Oberlieutenant's household. She seduced Gerda and made both the naïve mother and fragile 15-year-old daughter her sex slaves.

While Elsie scribbled in her diaries about romantic fantasies with handsome soldier boys, Gerda laid dreamy-eyed in Anita's bed in the adjoining room, hoping for tender caresses and orgasmic union with the German vamp. The love-struck mother proclaimed that she was willing to sacrifice everything for the attentions from her lesbian companion. But Anita had sexual feelings only for Gerda's daughter.

One morning, after a night of barhopping and nightclubbing, Gerda and Anita stumbled home in an alcoholic daze. Enraged at Anita's nonstop slutty escapades with the swarm of gamblers and high-steppers who followed the women through their jaunt, Gerda lunged at her lover, scratching her forehead and tearing off her white evening gown. Anita pushed her jealous sidekick away from their hotel bed and picked up a riding crop. She viciously beat Gerda down to the floor and, in a victorious bellow, ordered her drunken interloper to awaken Elsie and bring the girl into the room. Gerda kissed Anita's feet and sobbed hysterically, "Leave Elsie out of this." But Anita's whip had thoroughly transformed the grown woman into a frightened and submissive hound. Gerda groveled before the cruel mistress and begged for forgiveness and understanding. Anita stood aloof and triumphant with a riding crop in her hand.

Soundly defeated, Gerda rose and pounded on her daughter's door. Elsie shook with terror as she was led into the bridal suite. There the 15-year-old witnessed the primal scene of her mother's depraved sex obsession and Anita's power to humble all mortals within her hyper-erotic reach. That morning, all three, each in their own way, had lost their sense of petit-bourgeois honor and innocence.

While the Dresden Madonna fixed her white mask and applied new layers of eyeliner, a local doctor was summoned. The taciturn physician dressed Gerda's wounds and later contacted Elsie's father. The story of the scandalous incident at the Hotel Bristol preceded the dancer's return to Berlin. The legend of Anita Berber had taken yet another shocking turn.

Anita Berber Portfolio **by Charlotte Berend, 1919**

⚜ A PORNOGRAPHIC VISION ⚜

Charlotte Berend in 1906 achieved considerable fame as the first female artist to be inducted into the celebrated Berlin Session movement. His student for several years, and later the wife, of the celebrated painter Lovis Corinth, Berend proved to be a superior book illustrator and lithographist. Much in demand, her specialty was portraits of actors and dancers in theatrical settings. As her elderly husband's health deteriorated toward the end of the war, Berend sought more daring subjects and uncensored, contemporary outlets. In the spring of 1919, she invited Anita to her Berlin studio.

This page and opposite: *Anita Berber Portfolio* **by Charlotte Berend, 1919**

Berend sketched eight canvases of the decadent dance personality. Each picture captured Anita in a new and more provocative pose. There was the terrified child in a short hoop-skirt which fell just below her navel, directing the viewer's eye straight to the startled figure's exposed vagina and lower torso; the smiling adolescent, bagging her nightgown from top and bottom, to display her boyish breasts as well as her pubic hair and a single silk stocking; the confident fashion-plate sprawled across a chair; the inviting whore, sensationally naked except for an open black overcoat, rolled-up stockings, and high-heeled pumps; the saucy revue-girl at her makeup table, tonguing a phallic-looking

oyster; a hard-faced dancer, in Parisian attire, expertly pleasuring herself with her right leg thrown over the arm of a chair; a beckoning bride, wearing only dark hosiery, in a curtained chamber room; and a naked, open-mouthed showgirl, seated on her fur wraps.

The Gurlitt Gallery Press privately printed 80 luxurious sets of the "Anita Berber Portfolio" in the summer of 1919. Berend hand-painted and signed 40 of the oversized lithographic parcels and assumed that because of their fantastic cost and tiny run the series would probably elude Berlin's hard-pressed censoring boards. She was wrong. The entire Portfolio was labeled pornographic and quickly suppressed. Ten years later, the drawings reappeared in Viennese erotic encyclopedias and moral histories of the period. They would be among the most enduring images of Anita Berber between the time of her death and the beginning of Nazi rule.

❧ BETWEEN SATAN AND DEATH ☙

In June, Oswald reassembled three of his most marketable performers, Veidt, Reinhold Schünzel, and Anita, for another motion-picture novelty: a five-part anthology of individual horror sketches, entitled *Tales of the Macabre*. Based on stories by Anselm Heine, Robert Liebmann, Edgar Allen Poe, Robert Louis Stevenson, and Oswald himself, *Tales* juxtaposed dark and eccentric occult themes to uncover the mysterious links between forbidden desire, criminality, ghostly vengeance, and death. The discrete and genre-leaping format also showcased the stars' skill in portraying a variety of character types and ability to work in contrasting styles.

The introductory scene of *Tales* combined a framing device common to both the cabaret-revue and scenic Expressionism. Still images of the Devil, Death, and a prostitute hung from the wall in an old bookstore. At the stroke of midnight, the portraits smirked to one another and magically stepped out of their two-dimensional wall panels. Searching for a bit of grisly amusement, they browsed through the shop's tattered volumes and read appropriate passages aloud. Each of their selections was an episode in Oswald's script.

Conrad Veidt, Anita, and Reinhold Schünzel in *Tales of the Macabre*, 1919

Heine's grotesquerie "The Apparition" set the weird and paranoiac filmic mood. Anita played "the Mysterious Woman," whom a stranger (Veidt) invites to stay at his Parisian hotel. Claiming illness, she remains in her room but when the stranger awakens the next day, his curious guest has utterly disappeared. No one in the hotel can recall seeing them together or find any traces of her sojourn in her room, or her crafty exit. The night clerk maintains that it would be impossible for anyone to escape his practiced eye. Maybe the stranger only hallucinated his companion's existence. In a confused rage, Veidt paces the back alleys of Paris. Hours later, he spies a funeral procession. Inside the open coffin is his Mysterious Woman, another victim of a galloping plague. The entire city, including its hotel attendants, is determined to hush up the exact extent of the lethal contagion. The stranger then realizes he too had been infected and expires in a spasmodically slow and painful collapse.

In Liebmann's "The Hand," two men-about-town (Veidt and Schünzel) meet in a nightclub and both fall in madly love with the same dancer (Anita). The young men shake dice to see who will romance the beauty. Veidt wins but the lust-smitten Schünzel refuses to abide by the fateful toss. He strangles his friend and runs away. Years later, Anita

Tales of the Macabre, 1919

encounters the old Schünzel. That evening, he accompanies her to her grand debut in a cabaret. As the dancer performs a flirty Arabesque, Schünzel notices something bizarre on the edge of the backdrop: a disembodied claw and then a lurking shadow of his strangled friend. Schünzel faints in his box seat. After the show, Anita implores her pale-faced friend to attend a séance. And it is there that the bloody hand and its vengeful spirit-body reappears to murder the guilt-ridden Schünzel.

Adapted from Poe's short story, "The Black Cat" was more standard mystery hokum. A jealous husband (Schünzel) brings home an itinerant stranger (Veidt) whom he has befriended in a local tavern. The traveler is immediately attracted to the man's wife (Anita) and the husband secretly observes their flirtatious antics at the dinner table. As soon as the stranger departs, Schünzel smashes a beer stein over his vivacious wife's head, instantly killing her. He entombs her corpse in a cellar wall. But when the traveler returns the next day, the nervous husband shoos the man away, explaining his wife is off on a journey. Ever suspicious, the stranger has the police search the house for evidence of foul play. In the basement, they hear scratching sounds and break open the wall. Out leaps a black cat and the body of its murdered mistress.

Oswald's fourth episode, "The Suicide Club," was the only story without a Berber character. Schünzel plays an undercover London policeman, investigating the covert activities of the unusual gentlemen's society. He loses the game of Russian roulette, the club's *raison d'état*, but manages to outwit its president and stay alive.

The final episode, "The Ghost," was Oswald's comic afterword. A bored Baroness (Anita) takes an injured gentleman (Schünzel) into her castle. The Baron (Veidt) listens uncomfortably as the stranger regales his impressionable wife with personal tales of his stellar bravery and manliness. Feigning business duties, the Baron pretends to leave the following evening. But he returns later in ghostly attire, which scares his guest to flee the haunted environs. The Baron then unhoods himself before his frightened spouse, who sits in the Baron's lap and laughs hysterically at the elaborate hoax and her vanished hero.

When *Tales of the Macabre* premiered at the Berlin Bioscope Filmtheater, Oswald had finally achieved one of his long-stated goals: the formation of his private cinema empire, a string of upscale, Moorish-styled filmhouses across Germany. The celebration began on November 6th, with a live prologue written specially for Oswald and his acting stable. Anita traded a bit of slutty repartee with her co-stars and then performed an Arabesque ballet piece.

The Berlin press' response to *Tales* was uniformly glowing. Nearly every critic found some artistic aspect in Oswald's innovative bundle—the storytelling, alteration of performance modes, scenic design, costuming—to crow about. *Der Film* (#45, November 9, 1919) singled out Anita for her steadfast "charm and mature ability." The enthusiasm from local moviegoers was equally encouraging.

Not discussed in the reviews or elsewhere was any apparent meaning in the anthology's success. The placement of stories in *Tales* seemed nearly random or emotionally jumbled. Yet, a greater master narrative could be ferreted out of the five-part structure: it was Oswald's description of contemporary Weimar morality.

The first episode mocked the death of sexless innocence (the Wilhelmian era resituated in Paris); the second and third episodes revealed the life-in-death power of female sexuality (the world of Weimar); the fourth heralded the moral superiority and craftiness of the life force (in a universalized London); the fifth proclaimed the glory of horrific make-believe as a restorative for social harmony and happiness (in Oswald's modern Germany).

⊱ BERLIN'S GIRL-OF-THE-HOUR ⊰

The real-life Anita did not play according to the amusing or tragic rules laid out in Oswald's amoral comedies and erotic epics. Anita's manic behavior, beginning sometime in the summer of 1919, spun ever downward, with no obvious bottom in sight. Like much of bohemian Berlin, she experimented with drugs and participated in a host of late-night orgies.

An astonishing menu of illicit narcotics, smuggled from Hamburg and Paris, were traded and hawked in Berlin's Friedrichstadt cabaret district, Anita's newest playground. It was said that she loaded her indelicate bloodstream daily with hashish and opium fumes, morphine injections, cocaine powders, absinthe, and a chloral hydrate-ether concoction (ingested by biting white rose petals that were swirled in the crystalline solution). Among Anita's noted sexual partners then was the staid founder of German Sexology, Dr. Hirschfeld, previously thought to be exclusively gay and vehemently monogamous. (He later confided that the only female that he had sexual contact with was "the dancer" Anita Berber.)

In these early, unfettered years of Weimar, Anita was Berlin's most widely discussed female personality. German men's magazines, like *Reigen*, *Junggeselle*, *Berliner Leben*, *Die Ohne*, *Der Kavalier*, and *Galantes Leben*, never seemed to pass up an opportunity to include a drawing, photograph, poem, or implausible story about the winsome vamp. Typically, the New Years' or Fasching issue featured a salacious Anita Berber item or paean in their inside cover. For editors and designers, this skinny, half-blind, outré performer was the living avatar of their open city.

ANITA

by Erwin Erich Torenburg

With your shimmering clothes

And flowing hair,

Dance the Circle of Lust

For me, Anita.

With a crimson crown

Of rose petals and

A swelling breast,

Dance, Anita.

You, a beauty beyond compare,

Dance and spin.

Your youthful shape

Pries from me more

Than praise-worthy thoughts.

You steal my soul.

So, dance the Circle of Lust,

Anita, with your flowing hair,

And shimmering clothes.

Tear the buds

From the crimson flowers and

Press them to your

Young, swelling breast.

—*Der Junggeselle* (#13, January 1921)

From 1919 until her death, Anita's chief intoxicants were cocaine and cognac. These energized her and fueled her promiscuous encounters. In addition, she impulsively spent her considerable earnings on gaudy jewelry, imported furs and shoes, and a bizarre menagerie of eccentric pets. Anita's walk-up suite at the Hotel Adlon was her place of worship. There in her hellishly darkened boudoir, she displayed her beasts and arranged her assemblage of fetish objects: Gothic and Baroque statuettes, horseshoes, scraps of lingerie, buttons, assorted esoterica, and countless icons of Mary and Jesus.

According to the Czech choreographer Joe Jencik, this is where Anita staged her best and most truthful performances: "A wax-colored white face without eyebrows or eyes, her body lay on the bed, or sometimes in the bathtub, with a whip in her hand, ostrich feathers on her head, a red corset on her back, cocaine on her tongue, morphine under her skin, passed out from cognac. Anita's witnesses hid under the bed, under carpets, secreted their bodies behind the drapes. Men, women, children, adults, old, healthy, crippled were flogged and raped and enslaved in her name." (*Anita Berberová: Studie*, Prague: Terpsichora, 1930)

In the winter of 1919, Anita made her midnight excursions into the lobbies of Berlin's grand hotels and elegant restaurants looking like a drugged-out Eve. She stood by the foyer doorways naked except for a sable coat, high-heel pumps, a frightened baby chimpanzee hanging from her neck and an heirloom silver brooch, packed with cocaine. Her favorite stunt involved shocking unsuspecting maître d's when she requested their assistance in removing her outer wraps. The sudden exposure of her nude torso, made even more radiant and glowing through the application of opulent skin crèmes, together with the shriek from her body-warmed, sleepy pet, must have stunned more than the old, seen-it-all waiters. One unusually chilly evening, however, Anita felt the leathery hands around gaunt shoulders go cold; her beloved chimp had suffocated under its mistresses' numerous layers of clothing. Anita fell into a deep depression that no known stimulant could chemically remedy. She returned to her mother's apartment on Zähringer Strasse.

❧ DANCING DOLL ❧

Despite its reputation for freewheeling erotic spectacle, postwar censorship in the Prussian capital was haphazard and often bordered on the nonsensical. Anita could perform naked in any Friedrichstadt cabaret space because the vice-commissioners reasoned that paying customers expected such fare. But nudity and allusions to nonmarital sex in the traditional proscenium theatres in Berlin was another matter entirely. And, naturally, where there was scandal, there was also Fräulein Berber.

Arthur Schnitzler's blackout farce *Reigen* ("The Merry-Go-Round") about the hidden erotic chain that fantastically linked Hapburgian Vienna's social strata (from maids to counts) had a celebrated history, long before its suppression in Weimar Berlin. Written in 1897 and banned three years later in both Austro-Hungary and Imperial Germany, the play—like Oscar Wilde's *Salomé*—had acquired a variety of extra-cultural meanings. Critics wrote that it attacked both the communal fabric of Emperor Josef's world and, more significantly, its codes of honor. Some scenes of *Reigen* were considered relatively innocuous and permitted to be staged here and there; other episodes (especially those involving promiscuous females) were strictly forbidden.

Dr. Wilhelm Borchard was determined to be the first director to stage an up-to-date dramatization of *Reigen* in Berlin. If bucking the censors weren't enough to ensure an audience, he had a second strategy: put that Berber creature onstage in all her corporal allure. In August, Borchard's orgiastic vision opened at the properly named Phantastische Theater but he had managed only to mount a handful of Schnitzler's scenes. Anita appeared as a walk-on. She had little to do but to drop her red fan, unbutton her spangly dress, and then saunter across the proscenium as a naked-as-a-jaybird prostitute.

Journalists generally ignored the production and Anita's cursory presence. Borchard's cabaret-like presentation seemed trifling and deflected the larger issue regarding the suppression of staged literary works and legal definitions of "immorality." Spectators,

Pritzel Figurines at the Schall und Rauch Cabaret by Paul Erkens, 1920

however, flocked to the Neuen Kantstrasse theatre in anticipation of the feckless dancer's simple mimicry in Scene Five.

Four months later, a professional production of *Reigen* opened at the Kleines Schauspielhaus. This display could not be tolerated by the authorities and was forcibly closed after two weeks. The director, Hubert Reusch, and his producers were charged with multiple violations of Paragraphs 183 and 184, the Prussian statutes outlawing obscene acts on the legitimate theatre. Court proceedings began in August 1921 and Reusch was found guilty. He achieved the kind of infamy based on state hypocrisy that Schnitzler had set out to upend.

The Austrian impresario Max Reinhardt responded to the Berlin cabaret/theatre imbroglio by establishing the Schall und Rauch cabaret as an appendage to his massive Grosses Schauspielhaus in Berlin North. Reinhardt conceived of Schall as an intimate literary nightclub, but it had constant problems determining who its audience was and what its attractions ought to be. For its premiere production in December 1919, a Dada puppet show, *Simply Classical*, childishly parodied the master director's theatricalist *Orestia*, playing in the Schauspielhaus above.

By the spring of 1920, Schall's program resembled that of a Jägerstrasse dive. Berber did a star turn in April, performing "La Masque," "Pritzel Doll," and the "Caprice Espagnol." How many monthly presentations of Berber dances followed the April show is difficult to assess but the *Schall und Rauch* magazine included satirical line-drawings of her nude dances in their November and December issues. In any case, Anita had made an indelible showing among Reinhardt's theatrical elite. Other experimental artists quickly affixed themselves to the rising sensation.

Two young composers, Jaap Kool, a Dutch avant-gardist, and Mischa Spoliansky, an irrepressible revue showman, wrote special musical pieces for Anita's growing dance repertoire. Kool's serialized composition "Profane" was an attempt to impose ritual Dutch East Indies rhythms into a pseudo-American jazz score. Spoliansky jettisoned primitive or high culture influences altogether;

La Masque by Paul Erkens, 1920

he created a "hot tango" for Anita called "Morphine." This music was worth recording on shellac disks and could be heard in any of Berlin's dozen huge dance parlors. "Morphine" became an instant orchestral pop hit, a standard for at least five years.

The December 1920 cover of the Galante monthly *Reigen* displayed Anita in her prostitute getup from the Phantastische Theater production. Sitting on a cushy globe and laughing, the color figure of Anita kicked up her legs. In miniature, the scene from Schnitzler's *Reigen* could be read in full.

At the tail end of 1920, still another image of Anita appeared in women's journals and at art emporiums. Porcelain figures of her posing as the angular Korean Dancer and a bright-

Pierotte porcelain by Constantin Holzer-Defani, 1920

eyed Pierotte were mass-manufactured by the Rosenthal Selb firm in Bavaria. Sculpted by the Viennese artist Constantin Holzer-Defani, these costly hand-painted models were sold alongside those of Anna Pavlova and only a few other divas of Terpsichore. In the imagination of Germany's tastemakers, Anita (in her teenage incarnations) had joined the ranks of the internationally recognized and aesthetically fashionable.

SHAMELESS ⋙ DAUGHTER ⋘

Anita's controversial, if minute, theatrical performance did little to derail her acting career or her ability to entrance audiences. In 1920 and 1921, she appeared in six more films doing femme-fataleish cameos. In Oswald's *Night Figures* (January 1920), she played Nella, a sullen tightrope-dancer who leaves the richest man in the world, eventually causing his psychological downfall. In another Oswald costume weepie, *The Count of Cagliostro* (January 1921), her role was further reduced to that of a second- or third-tier lead, Lorenza, Cagliostro's sometime lover.

Anita Berber, to be sure, had high name recognition but her cocaine and alcohol addiction made her a creative liability on the set.

During the shooting of *The Shame of the Pharaoh's Daughter* in August 1920, the director Otz Tollen had to deal with Anita's implacable temperament. Not only was she

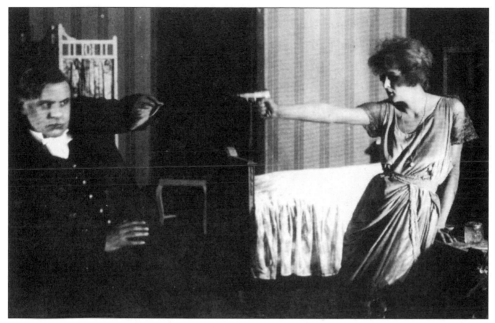

Shame of the Pharaoh's Daughter, 1920

argumentative, erratic, and constantly late, the girl also was a danger to his staff. When the prop man mistakenly left a live round in the chamber of a stage pistol, Anita grabbed the errant weapon and promptly fired the bullet into the man's thigh.

Under any normal circumstance, Anita would have been physically removed from the studio set or immediately replaced, but Tollen quietly demurred; he was a fellow in the dancer's intimate circle of sexual devotees. Fourteen years her senior, Tollen once asked Anita if she could be attracted to an older man like him. The vamp replied with a shrug, "Of course, but, you know, I prefer younger women."

Tollen's wife, Maria Merlott, supposedly an impartial observer, never forgot spying a sensational scene of Anita in her snow-white makeup at the Königin-Bar. It was a pick-up joint for dashing young officers on the make. Interrupting their vain, if practiced, attempts to outdo one another in impressing her, the starlet screamed in her cognac-induced boredom, "Shut up! I will sleep with all of you!"

Anita's marriage, never a model of bourgeois probity, had soured completely by 1920. Von Nathusius, of course, had given his wife a wide berth, sometimes accompanying

Susi Wandowski and Anita, 1922

her in Friedrichstadt sexcapades; finally, over a two-year period of nonstop infidelities, she withdrew completely. By the time the town gossips had traded all the giggly details about the *Pharaoh's Daughter* affair, the sex kitten had lost interest in men entirely. Anita declared herself a confirmed lesbian. She had already dated a swarm of pansexual beauties, like the vivacious chorine Marlene Dietrich and the pouty starlet Lya de Putti. At the end of the year, Berlin's wild child settled on Susi Wanowski, the owner of the Comobar, a classy lesbian Lokal on Kommandanstrasse.

Anita hired Susi to be her manager and secretary and, after a few months, her primary sex partner. At the Hotel Esplanade, another scandal ensued. Anita confronted Susi's husband and son about her sacred lesbian vows with Frau Wandowski. Despite Susi's protests, Anita had the Wanowski males thrown into the street. The much-tormented von Nathusius had enough and filed for divorce.

In Vienna, where Anita's starry aura still shone brightly, a lovesick baroness, Leonie Puttkamer-Gessmann, wrote the glam girl a series of suggestive fan letters and telegrams. The mash notes hinted that both were from the same Hot Sister sorority. Leonie, like Susi, was a top-girl. She knew how to excite both the male and female—with whips, fetishistic humiliation, and smacks to the bare buttocks. Susi destroyed the smutty invitations. It was the last thing their fragile relationship needed. Three months later, in July 1921, the star and her protective manager vacationed in the spa town of Karlsbad.

The Baroness tracked them down and followed the duo there. Leonie had a plan: entice her masochistic husband, the Baron Albert Gessmann, to introduce himself to Anita as an interested aesthete; after a few drinks, the old baron could then offer to contact a friend, the director of the hoity-toity Viennese nightclub, the Tabarin, for a lucrative dance engagement. Anita would soon be in Vienna, in Leonie's bed, the baroness prayed, beneath the cherished photograph of the naked dancer she kept by her nightstand.

Leonie failed to make contact with Anita in Karlsbad. Afterward the dizzy aristocrat attempted to persuade her husband to go to Berlin, where he could do his business and she could do hers. Gessmann rejected the notion. Leonie and her obsessive lesbian schemes were more controllable at home. At his urging, the Tabarin director later wrote Susi about an exclusive Berber production; unfortunately, the vixen-girl's schedule in Berlin was already overbooked.

None of these high-lifers, evidently, paid much attention to the stalled international conferences in Versailles that harshly recalculated Germany's war reparations and the monetary earthquake that was about to swallow Central Europe.

MORE STAGE, MORE SCREEN, ⋙ AND A BOOK ⋘

The Great Inflation that thoroughly altered German mores and requisite amusements did not have much affect on Anita's outlook or performance activities. She still played in films, although most would be minor Viennese three-hankie soaps. (Typically, she starred in the 1921 kitschy *Destroyed Life* as a Heidi-gone-wrong character, who dies

Anita Berber as Eton-Boy in *Please Pay!* by Ernst Schneider, 1921

while searching for her brother in the big city.) The wild antics associated with Anita's savage and unpredictable personality predated the Inflation era. But there seemed to be a new cultural justification for them, and other dancers were following in her silk-clad footsteps.

In October 1921, the first images of Anita outside Europe appeared in the American periodical *Vanity Fair*. She was identified as one "the Screen Actresses Who Distract the Troubled Capitals of Central Europe." Curiously, D'Ora illustrated her film work with two photographs from her old Blüthner-Saal dances, "Caprice Espanol" and "Heliogabal." Most likely, they were selected because of their artistic quality and format.

From the middle of October until early November 1921, Anita performed in Rudolf Nelson's topical revue, *Please Pay!* An old friend of Lucie and Fritz Grünbaum, Nelson needed something *au courant* for his sendup of money-mad, anything-goes-Berlin. Anita was perfect. In "Making Perversions," she came onstage in a bowler hat, monocle, elegant smoking jacket, and loose-fitting pants. Her number "We're Standing Backwards" concluded with a hip-rattling shimmy performed on a glass table that was illuminated from below. The critics swooned over the act. One of them described Anita's movements as an improbable "blend of grace and depravity."

In the audience was Fritz Lang, the autocratic Expressionist filmmaker. He had little interest in Anita as an actor or celebrity. Lang needed some decadent filler for his next grand opus, *Mabuse, the Great Gambler*. He contacted Susi and offered Anita the part of Aud Egede-Nissen's double for Cara Carozza, a revue-dancer from the Folies Bergère.

According to Erich Kettelhut, Lang's set designer and futurist architect, the no-nonsense director came to regret his casting choice. Not only was Lang ignorant of Anita's onscreen career, he evidently knew nothing about her temperamental ego, drug addictions, or unruly behavior on the set.

On the day Anita was to be filmed in November 1921, she appeared at the Neubabels-berg studio two hours late. In his 600-page unpublished memoir, Kettelhut comically

She From the Circus, 1922

recalled Lang's response. The imperious director had been waiting impatiently with his idle crew, hopping from leg to leg, constantly peering out the studio door. When Anita's taxi finally arrived, Lang attempted to be gallant. He opened the taxi door and politely inquired about the reason for her tardiness. Anita waved him away. She had been partying until eight that morning and required some hours to fix her less-than-stellar appearance. She also expected Lang to pick up her inflationary cab fare.

Hoping to rescue the costly and insulting diversion, Lang swallowed his Prussian pride and continued to treat the bratty stripper like royalty. He courteously guided Anita to the makeup and costume rooms. According to Kettelhut, the entire staff was taken with the girl's bizarre devil-may-care attitude and shockingly beautiful, if underdeveloped, body. When Lang demanded that Anita's thick, blonde pubic hair be shaved, the crazed dancer adamantly protested. A patch of flesh-toned artificial skin had to be cut and glued to Anita's genital region in order to mask the cinematically offending hairs. The old wardrobe man visibly shook as he applied the triangular mat to the amoral dancer's lower torso.

Anita's first scene had her prance merrily between two gigantic noses at either end of the imaginary proscenium stage. An electric wind fan then blew Carla's floppy hat and black dress into the wings. Covering her naked breasts with a tiny hand, Anita coyly bowed as the olio curtain fell.

The revue-dancer's second scene took place in Mabuse's secret casino. Anita merely reprised her "Making Perversions" routine. Resplendent in a tight-fitting tuxedo, Anita shuffled atop a miniature round platform that magically overturned into an empty gambling table. Anita completed her part, most of which was dumped into the censor's waste bin.

Christmas 1921 saw the first *roman à clef* about Anita, *Die Tänze der Ina Raffay* [*The Dances of Ina Raffay*] (Berlin: Verlag Ullstein, 1921). Written by the up-and-coming Viennese novelist Vicki Baum, it told the tragic story of a sweet but increasingly disturbed red-haired erotic dancer. In its last few pages, Ina Raffay, despite the admiration of powerful male sycophants, dies at 25 on her mother's bed, lonely and artistically unfulfilled.

❧ INFLATION QUEEN ☙

While the Inflation deepened in the winter and spring months of 1922, Anita's fame continued to rise. *Shadowland*, an oversized American art and stage magazine which heralded the transatlantic flapper aesthetic, featured the Central European star in its January

Anita Berber **by Knut Honsen,** *Der Junggeselle,* **April 1922**

issue. Produced, directed, and scripted by William Kahan, another Viennese film melodrama staring Anita as a fiery tightrope dancer, *She From the Circus* opened in March. One month after that, Anita performed naked, in veils, and as a sad-faced Pierrotte at the 99-seat Weisse Maus cabaret, where fun-seeking Berlin spectators were given half-masks to conceal their identities. Mostly the audience swilled champagne and groped one another while the determined artiste leaped across the 16-foot stage.

No one captured Anita's place in the Inflation madness more unsparingly than the peripatetic Viennese-Jewish writer and permanent outsider, Leo Lania (born Hermann Lazar). Arriving in the Babylon-on-the-Spree, after receiving a coveted interview with Benito Mussolini, Italy's freshly anointed strongman, Lania was amazed at his poor timing. There was little freelance work in the Berlin publishing world just then; one editor after another claimed German readers were bored by such international fluff that Lania so excelled in unearthing.

One balmy May night in 1922, after another frustrating odyssey seeking a secure literary post or some temporary employment, Lania scouted out the wicked Friedrichstadt. It was well past midnight but the streets there were still flooded with hundreds of lowlife peddlers and barkers, dolled-up hookers, their equally made-up and garish-looking younger brothers, pickpockets, beggars, smirking pimps and an endless stream of gawkers and willing clientele.

In front of boarded-up food shops, pornographic postcards, drugs, matches, and black-market currency were gamely traded. Blackboards (with crossed-off numbers) graphically showed how the value of the mark had sunk by the quarter-hour. Policemen, shouldering rifles, largely ignored the fetid swamp of criminal activity. They were concerned only with threats of looting and political roughhousing, some of which had taken place during the daylight hours.

In the Passage, a notorious lair for boy-prostitution, a portrait of the Kaiser was flanked by photos of "documents of female beauty," naked women. A few steps farther down was the Anatomical Wonder Cabinet. On its storefront window, a sign was pasted: "No children admitted."

As Lania stepped along, a schlepper for a naked revue attempted to push aside a throaty war cripple. The legless hawker struggled to flash his artificial limbs under the streetlight as a further inducement for potential customers. Sales in the form of charity; charity in the form of sales. But his competition, the living cabaret poster, promised visual delights. "Guaranteed naked women. Naked to the skin. See them tonight! Guaranteed!"

Out of nowhere, a woman interrupted the man's practiced spiel. The words she used were so rude, so indecent that the schlepper recognized her from her choice vocabulary. He fell silent for a moment and acknowledged her exalted presence with a servile nod. He greeted her simply as "Anita."

Lania studied the scene; maybe there was a story in it. The picture-perfect woman wore a pricey black fur coat and across her wrists and neck were strings of flawless jewels. Beneath her flaming red hair, she sported a monocle that covered one eye. The underworld priestess had just exited a restaurant with a pack of men close behind. Passersby stopped in their tracks to get a better view; even the whores watched in awe. Acolytes in the

The Three Maries and the Mister From Marana, 1922

crowd formed a protective corridor so their idol could reach the door of her chauffeured limousine unscathed.

Alfred Beierle, a Reinhardt actor whom Lania knew from the Romanisches Café, was among Anita's party. He invited the fascinated journalist to come along. Once inside the automobile, the self-assured beauty acted like Lania was an old, trusted valet. She dropped a gold mesh purse into his hand and told him to hold on to it. In her drunken lethargic confusion, Anita explained, she was always losing her handbags. This night she would remember to appoint a retainer.

"Involuntarily I opened the pocketbook, it contained a thick bundle of banknotes, many of them American. I closed it and obediently thrust it into my pocket. That was my [first] meeting with Anita Berber." (*Today We Are Brothers*, Boston: Houghton Mifflin Co., 1942)

In June, Vienna beckoned once again. Anita played a Renaissance swinger in Schünzel's film *The Three Maries and the Mister From Marana*. It was set in fifteenth-century Paris but obviously spoke to twentieth-century concerns.

Baroness Leonie Puttkamer-Gessmann could not contain herself. If anything, her desire to be with Anita had intensified dramatically over the year since Karlsbad. In desperation, Leonie telephoned every chic hotel near the film quarter. Again her sleuthing paid off. She discovered that Anita and Susi were staying at the Parkhotel in Hietzing.

Anita had neither the time nor any compelling interest in the Baroness' antics. But Leonie (or Leo, as Vienna's femmes knew her) was not deterred. The erotic storm that rumbled inside her could not be calmed. The relentless aristocrat took up residence nearby and waited—in vain, at first—for Anita to show up at some seedy corner lesbian bar or plush hotel lobby. Finally, they made contact. Behind the backs of the Baron and Susi, the absurd duo of cold-and-hot-lovers had an encounter. It lasted one week.

For Anita, the affair with Leonie was nothing, unmemorable, one of many hundreds of on-the-road flings. For the baroness, it was quite a different experience. She invited the naked dancer to the Gessmann mansion for a late-night dinner. Leonie did not hide her erotic entrancement from the baron. How could she? He calmly absented himself from the table and slept alone. Like Susi, the kindly eunuch fumed while Anita and Leonie fucked.

One evening after a long day's shoot, Anita sidestepped the baroness and went off with her co-star Bebi Becker (one of Schünzel's "Maries") to a cozy suite in the Hotel Bristol. This, for Anita, was a romance better worth pursuing. It was emotionally dead and therefore appealing. Leonie recoiled in shock.

The heartbroken baroness arranged to meet Susi at the Parkhotel and cautioned her about Anita's deleterious sex life. The dancer was destroying herself and everyone in her path. Susi brushed aside Puttkamer's warnings. Leonie decided to confront Anita directly. It utterly backfired. The ice-goddess sweet-talked the naïve woman into joining Susi, Bebi, and her for a madcap night on the town. Their affair lasted one week.

The soirees concluded in Bebi's suite. By the end of the month after final filming, Anita left both her Viennese starlet and Leonie. Some mysterious force was pulling the dancer back to her beloved Berlin. And like a shadow, Susi dutifully followed her home.

Baron Albert Gessmann divorced Leonie one month later. His lawyer presented all sorts of material that documented the baroness' perverse and adulterous activities to the municipal authorities. (i.e., after groveling at Leonie's booted feet, the baron was commanded to place his flaccid member between his wife's breasts. But which of them constructed this scenario of domestic debasement became a matter of legal dispute.) Letters and extensive transcriptions of Anita Berber's shameful proclivities were also entered into the public record.

The Viennese tabloids had a field day. Their yellow journalists tried to determine which city—Vienna or Berlin—had the most immoral inhabitants. Answers to that weighty inquiry would be issued before New Year's 1923.

CHAPTER FOUR
REPERTOIRE OF THE DAMNED
(1922–1923)

Anita despised all men, especially those who worshipped her mistress persona. She thought even less of women, particularly ladies who were titillated by her lesbian affairs. And she was equally bored with spectators who believed in her androgyny or the ambiguity of her sexual feelings. In "Astarte" Anita danced her true erotic sphere and sex: she was neuter and belonged to no one. No one could touch her or take her. She belonged only to herself and she alone was subject to the magnetism of her own sexual charge. Anita performed the goddess of the moon in human, female form. If Astarte ever existed, she was surely incarnated in this German dancer.

—Joe Jencik, *Anita Berberová: Studie* (Prague: Terpsichora, 1930)

❧ THE BOY-WOMAN DROSTE ❧

Sometime in the afterhours of April or May 1920, Sebastian Droste arranged to meet with Anita at the Schall und Rauch. He was a naked dancer and a featured member of the still-flourishing Celly de Rheidt ballet troupe. Droste had some small success as a choreographer and published Expressionist poetry and plays in Herwarth Walden's prestigious art journal *Der Sturm*. For the Schall's end-of-the-year extravaganza, the starlet and her male interloper briefly paired up and performed Spoliansky's "Dance of Morphine."

Eighteen months later, Anita played house in a walk-up with Dr. Heinrich Klapper, a determinedly lowlife physician whose principal means of support were illegal abortions for hookers and daughters of privilege. He was known throughout the Friedrichstadt simply as "The Stork." At that time, Anita Berber had her tightly defined circle of friends and hangers-on. They sniffed out the latest Lokals, sex emporiums, criminal dives, and private gambling dens. The latter were constantly raided and shuttered by the city's overworked "Bulls" only to resurface a few corners away.

Anita's one amusement that did not involve drugs or high-stake wagers was French cooking. In Klapper's apartment, she would rouse up her fellow cokeheads with plates of freshly prepared pastries and mayonnaise-topped crayfish and lobster. The drug-satiated crowd or

Sebastian Droste, 1920

the chef rarely consumed the gourmet dishes, but the tipsy naked dancer in high heels and sable wraps was a common sight in Berlin's open-at-dawn produce markets. A bit of Wilhelmian decorum in an otherwise messy and knockabout lifestyle.

On June 13th, 1922, Droste reintroduced himself to Anita in one of Berlin West's illicit casinos. There was no particular reason for Anita to recall or acknowledge the freaky upstart. Droste, she whispered to her companions, was one of a string of arrivistes and backstage Johans who accosted the diva nightly in her dressing room, at the stage door, and on the street. The Inflation Queen consigned such annoyances to Susi—unless they came with offerings of imported cognac or open tins of white powdered stimulants.

The life-shattering encounter was certainly on the thirteenth of the month because that was the number the crucifix-wearing redhead bet on repeatedly at the roulette table that very late evening. According to Lania's two differing accounts, Susi, Klapper, Beierle, and an

Anita by Johann Stremberg, *Reigen*, May 1921

amateur writer Hans M. accompanied the depraved princess to the newly refurbished gambling parlor.

Remarkably, Anita's bet on number 13 was a match twice in two tries. God had smiled on her, it seemed. Against all logic, she continued to play the primary number, placing more and more chips on the roulette table square. When she ran out of money and chips, Anita borrowed from her less blessed friends. But they too were about to go bust. The wheels of fortune spun against them.

Amidst all the tumult, the inebriated Anita picked up a chunky bronze ashtray and hurled it directly at the croupier's head. It sailed across the table, scattering cigar ashes everywhere, and struck the old man near his left eye. The force of the projectile, or just the shock, was powerful enough to knock him over. Finally the bratty loser had satisfaction. She laughed triumphantly while Klapper administered first aid to the croupier's bloody forehead.

Before Susi could usher her ward away, Droste took Anita's arm and led her down a back stairwell. They had much to talk about. This introduction Anita would remember. It gave new focus to her unsettled life and career.

Like Anita, Droste used cocaine to inspire his dancerly visions and possessed a cold-hearted, nearly inhuman, personality. Even his collaborators thought him vicious and self-serving. Yet as a solo nightclub performer or experimental writer, Droste had extremely limited talents. He had already exhausted his bodily arts that season. Now with Anita, he had a brand new spectrum of color and vibrations, a cabinet of exotic ingredients, a female Heliogabal.

No naked dancer was quite like Berber—not in appearance, not in reputation, not in raw talent. Anita attempted to incorporate episodes of her life onstage. She desired to include her solipsist religion, her strange little loves, and her dazzling craft in movement. She wanted each dance to have deep meaning, to encompass her demonic oeuvre. The goal was to make a permanent impression on her uncaring public. Anita only needed a like-minded partner and a skilled director to achieve that end.

The kohl-eyed Droste was her man. His sexual creepiness and ability to manipulate Berlin's seen-it-all showpeople elevated him to a very high plateau. To be sure, among the growing flock of smarmy hucksters and schemers who inundated that bleak environment, Droste was greatly accomplished and cunning. Anita could topple a croupier in his tracks, but her next manager and husband believed he could do the same to the warbling placards of Central Europe's avant-garde.

Droste and Anita snorted cocaine and brainstormed future evenings of decadent productions. They rehearsed at the Weisse Maus in the afternoons and got even higher. Anita had not rehearsed so much since the Pirelli days and she consumed so many drugs that she became visibly ill.

ADAM AND AN AILING EVE
⋙ COME TO VIENNA ⋘

Droste had now totally replaced Susi as Anita's business manager; he had grander visions, and—equally important, as her procurer of cocaine, morphine, and hashish—the man had better sources. In July, Droste concluded a fantastic contract at Vienna's Great Konzerthaus-Saal. The owner, Hugo Heller, knew a good attraction and booked them for three exclusive evenings, spaced out during November and December. Financially, the deal for Heller seemed immensely profitable; the mark was falling faster than the Austrian kroner. But the impresario had not factored in Droste's congenital need for monetary legerdemain and contractual duplicity.

Veidt and Anita in *Lucrezia Borgia*, 1922

With a full production in mind, Anita and Sebastian worked quickly. They called their program *The Dances of Depravity, Horror, and Ecstasy*. One half of the numbers, old hits, were already choreographed. Another six would have to be manufactured.

The drugs and heavy schedule took a toll on the fragile beauty. After five weeks, Anita shipped off to Vienna and checked into the Sanatorium Loew. Emotionally shot and frightened about the local reception to her Konzerthaus-Saal presentation, she opened the *Neues Wiener Journal* on October 4th and read that she had been institutionalized for a mental disorder and was being treated accordingly. Anita promptly issued a rejoinder to the nosy tabloid. She wrote that her hospitalization was due to colic or a chronic stomachache.

Karl Kraus, Vienna's leading cultural critic, reprinted the Berlinerinn's letter-to-the-editor in his monthly *Die Fackel* (#601, November). He added a sardonic afternote. Wasn't the mere fact that the dancer seriously responded to the muckraking daily documentary proof of her purported madness?

Old Viennese admirers of Anita visited her at the clinic on Mariannengasse in September and October. Leonie brought her current lesbian protégée, Sidonie Csillag, a demure Jewish intellectual from the countryside. Sidi took an immediate dislike to the dancer. She detested her vain, whiny personality and doubted her scenic skills as an innovator and cult performer. The exotic object of Leo's summer fling, in many ways, resembled the severely depressed inmates in the hospital's adjoining rooms. Each morning, Anita bounced from ragged despair to tedious megalomaniac heights.

On October 6th, Oswald's Renaissance epic film *Lucrezia Borgia* was released. Anita played the decadent countess Julia Orsini. The part was small—her last with Connie Veidt and Oswald—but it re-established her star potential.

Heller sighed with relief. Crazy or not, Anita was a real celebrity. Droste surfaced in Vienna on the 14th and whisked her away for two weeks to Italy, Spain, and Paris. In distant and third-rate nightclubs, they would perfect their evening of depravity without the jaundiced glare of a hostile press or art-spewing, skeptical public.

On October 29th, the couple returned to Vienna revitalized. Whatever happened on their mad-dash sojourn must have been felicitous. They were more than eager to present their outré evening.

The curtain for *Dances of Depravity* rose at 10:30 p.m. on November 14th. (Special streetcars had to be scheduled for the late-night spectators.) The sets were designed by the Viennese architect Harry Täuber and the costumes created by the Atelier K. Karasek. The event, advertised as a "Unique Evening of Dance," was less and—over time—more than Heller and Vienna's columnists could ever imagine.

THE DANCES OF DEPRAVITY, HORROR, ⋙ AND ECSTASY ⋘

1) "Pritzel Figurines" ('The Bajadere and Her Idol'): Curtain reveals the porcelain figure of a Bajadere (Anita), an Indian temple dancer, sitting on a table. Asiatic ritual music of Jaap Kool begins. A bare-chested Idol (Droste) makes mysterious mudras from the side of the stage. The Bajadere moves. She leaps off the table and pirouettes on a clear globe-like ball. Her delicate arms rise above her head as she pivots and twirls like a mechanical doll. The Bajadere stops when the Idol signals the music to conclude. The now living female

Pritzel figurines, Atelier Alex Binder and Atelier Eberth, 1922

"Byzantine Whip Dance" and "Cocaine," Atelier D'Ora, 1922

figure in sexy garb gives a defiant laugh by the left wing of the stage and disappears into the darkness. (It could be read as the symbolic story of the new Berber, the influence of her controlling lover, and their shared contempt for the Viennese *Feinsmeckers*.)

2) "Byzantine Whip Dance": A Byzantine entertainer (Droste) enters to the music of Robert Volkmann. He tears off his knotted scarf from around his neck and flagellates himself with it. His sadistic impulses take him around the stage, facing every direction.

3) "Cocaine": On an Expressionistic wooden table, a cocaine addict or abandoned prostitute (Anita) lays spread-eagle. A street lamp slowly brightens and flickers. It casts a faint eerie shadow of bluish-grey. It could be dusk or dawn. The orchestra plays Camille Saint-Saëns' *Valse mignonne*. The addict awakens. She is in great pain. Her body trembles

and spasms. She holds her aching head for a moment and edges off the slab. The whore turns upstage, with her leather-corseted back to the audience. Mechanically she looks left in profile. The woman then spins madly, trying to break free of the drug's spell. In spurts, she attempts to stretch her limbs and plant her body in a secure spot but she shakes terribly. Twirling unsteadily to the corner like a stringed marionette, the addict stops abruptly. Then she places her hands behind her neck. The prostitute's bare, unnaturally white breasts radiate white-hot desire. Just as slowly as she arose from the table, the cocaine addict collapses to the floor, facing

"Cocaine," Atelier D'Ora, 1922

downward. The poison has defeated her. A soul has slipped over into the abyss.

4) "Martyr": Tied to a post with sharpened spikes, the nearly naked Saint Sebastian (Droste) looks to heaven. While the First Movement of Sergei Rachmaninov's *Symphonic Dances* plays, he suffers the torment of imaginary arrows striking his body. Each arrow produces a reaction. Only his arms and face register the pain. He signals his distress to a silent deity. The saint starts to expire, not knowing if

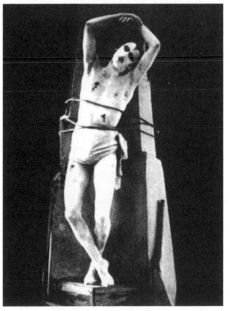

"Martyr" film still from *Modern Dances*, 1922

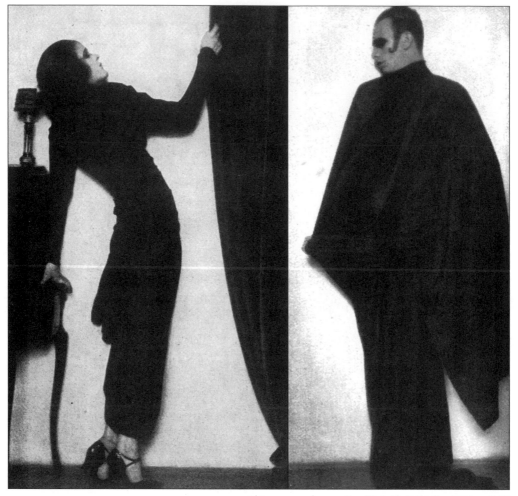

This page and opposite: "Suicide," Atelier D'Ora, 1922

his sacrifice has been witnessed or sanctified. Finally he hears bells from above. His martyrdom is accepted.

5) "Suicide": A Man (Droste) and a Prostitute (Anita) in black silk pajamas enter uncertainly from either side of the stage. They are in a modern bedroom. Playfully she steps to him. The concert pianist Otto Schulhof plays Ludwig von Beethoven's *Moonlight Sonata*. They touch. Then she falls to her knees, sliding her hand down the trim of his black cape. The mood has changed. Putting a hand to her neck, he stares at the Prostitute and methodically strangles her. In shock, he realizes that he is murdering his own soul. The Prostitute laughs. Blackout.

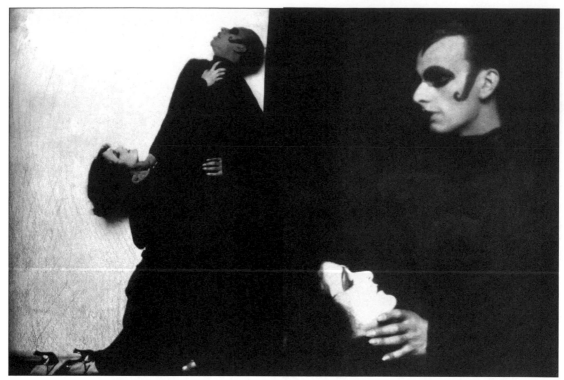

"Suicide," Atelier D'Ora, 1922

6) "Vision": A Nun in a white habit (Anita) walks across the stage in a trance. Beethoven's music guides her vision of a pure life. Her eyes shut in ecstatic devotion as she dreams of a union with her God. The woman has transformed herself into the Bride of Christ. Her ecstatic vision is fulfilled.

7) "Egyptian Prince": The son of the Pharaoh (Droste) enters the stage like a living hieroglyph image. Following the rhythm of a percussive drumbeat and the wails from a single flute, he marches across the stage floor, striking angular poses with his bent arms. He is the lord and high priest of his

"Vision," Atelier D'Ora, 1922

world. But the boy despises his exalted position and worldly privileges. He faces the audience and throws aside his golden crown in one impulsive movement. The Pharaoh's son falls to the floor, stroking his arms and body, which are covered with jewels—riches that generations of his ancestors acquired from slave labor. The prince hunches over and moans.

This page: "Egyptian Prince," József Pécsi, 1923

8) "Morphine": Deep in an old armchair sits a Woman dressed in a black clinging dress and a diaphanous cap (Anita). Around her neck is a golden jewel and on her hand a ring. She holds a syringe and stares at her forearm. She injects herself with the fluid. The music of Mischa Spoliansky's "Morphine" accompanies the drug rush into her body. For a while nothing moves, then she thrusts her body in an incredible arch, like a morbid rainbow. Vision after vision, the dancer moves in broken movements from one ecstatic position to another. She circles the chair. A Mona Lisa-like smile appears on the Woman's knowing lips. Then her face freezes into a Noh-like mask. She holds the stylized pose. A shudder passes

"Morphine," Atelier D'Ora, 1922

across her rigid body and she falls dead across the armchair. Her arched stomach points to the ceiling. Curtain.

9) "Lunatic Asylum": A Madman in a long green smock (Droste) attempts to escape from the lunatic asylum. He struggles to outrace a demon, his own masked shadow. To the theme of Rachmaninov's *Symphonic Dances*, he threatens the beast with insane roars and clenched fists. Wherever he turns, however, the shadow remains, his constant keeper and tormentor. There is no place on the stage free from the menacing shadow. He screams.

"Lunatic Asylum," Atelier D'Ora, 1922

10) "Astarte": The orchestra plays a Tchaikovsky interlude. Astarte (Anita) enters in a long silver cape. On her head is a silver helmet with undulating bunches of ostrich feathers. She wears a thin black mask. Like a silver cloud, she floats across the stage. Is it a woman? A boy? A great bird? It is Astarte. She gives out a piercing cry, then a bright laugh. Her cape falls off her shoulders. Her mask unfurls. Astarte's near-naked body blazes like a white flame on the stage. Stepping over the silver robe, she poses to the left and right. Laughingly, she shakes her upper torso. Just as quickly, she genuflects and holds up a palm. Slowly the untouchable Astarte covers her face. There she remains standing. Naked, hopeless. She shows nothing more in her face. Before the curtain falls, the sad-eyed goddess stoops to pick up her cape and remains still.

"Astarte," Atelier D'Ora, 1922

11) "Night of the Borgias": The Third Movement of Rachmaninov's *Symphonic Dances* introduces Lucrezia Borgia (Anita) to the audience. Her diaphanous wardrobe belongs to no time, no particular place, only the markings of royalty. Her arabesques also display a confident Italian aristocrat intent on a life of joy and freedom. She is still for a moment and a wave of fear suddenly registers on her face.

"Astarte" film still from *Light From the Depths*, 1922

Lucrezia glances stage left at an unseen terror. She removes her silk headband and slips out of her dress in despair. Her father, Caesar Borgia (Droste), approaches from stage left. He is nude, except for a white undergarment that covers his loins. Smiling and with her fingers linked behind her head, she crosses to him. He is in anguish. The naked daughter burns with incestuous desires. Lucrezia kneels and pulls her father down to the darkened stage floor. Blackout.

"Night of the Borgias,"
Atelier D'Ora, 1922

"Night of the Borgias," Atelier D'Ora, 1922

❧ SCANDAL AND FLIGHT ❧

Vienna's smart set, the city's dance critics, and Anita's coterie all attended the Konzerthaus-Saal opening. The performance went well but two reviewers got into a spat over the aesthetic quality and so-called offensive meaning of the piece. Despite her earlier misgivings, Sidi was greatly impressed with Anita's stage presence and emotional commitment. Like the critics, Sidi thought Droste a lesser talent. He could nowhere attain Anita's erotic fire. He was a competent mime at best.

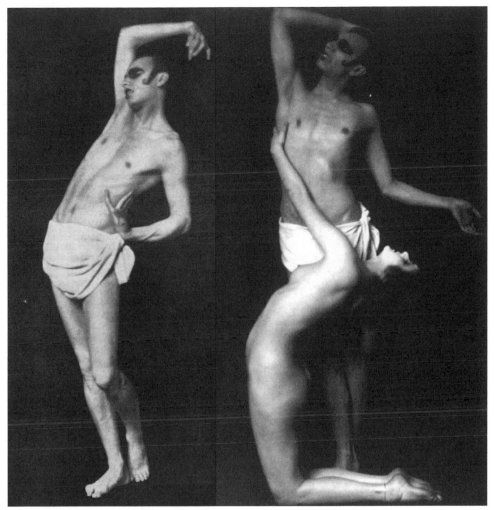

"Night of the Borgias," Atelier D'Ora, 1922

No reviews appeared for ten days.

"Around the Rialto"

Anita Berber is quite another story. The distinguished audience at the Konzerthaus found her an incontrovertible sensation. Her "dance" is a product of decay created from movement and mute, erotic signs; between radiating symbols of life-affirmance and the longing for death. The style of her degeneracy, which she reveals with great sincerity, manifests itself with her naked flesh—a wonderfully beautiful body of a moon-creature, so to speak—in a final stage moment. Anita's "dance" unveils the primal elements of our era: horror, fright, decadence, and waves of desire. Yes, waves of desire—I cannot help myself. Her partner, Herr Sebastian Droste, who strangles her to the sounds of Beethoven's Moonlight Sonata (what a pleasure!), is in no way an especially talented mimic. But he offered, in bronzed spurts, some striking moments.

> The spectators were enchanted and did not feel any noticeable discomfort. I
> felt abused when I saw the dance of the Moonlight Sonata and winced. It was like
> watching the entrails of a noble spirit ripped from the skillful hands of Otto Schulhof.
> Droste appeared to play it in an upbeat fashion in order to deny his complicity in the
> musical sacrilege.
> Couldn't the National Assembly pass a Beethoven Protection Law?
>
> —*Illustriertes Weiner Extrablatt* (November 24, 1922)

Since September, Droste and Anita had amassed a debt of 200 million kroner—largely due to Anita's hospitalization and evening extravaganzas as well as Droste's drug purchases and incidentals on the road. Previously in Germany, Droste's father had bailed out his prodigal son. But the German mark was worthless. Now Droste was on his own.

On November 15th, one day after the Konzerthaus performance, Droste attempted a new ruse: he convinced a gullible jeweler in the Graben district to loan him 50 million kroner. The oily confidence man presented a letter of credit signed by the Austrian Prince Taxis. Droste had befriended the prince during a nightly outing but the letter was phony and the aristocrat's signature forged. The next day, Droste was arrested for the outrageous swindle.

Droste's creditors urged the court to drop the suit. If their man was found guilty and deported, the Berber-Droste dance evenings would have to be cancelled and then there was no way they could recover their enormous losses. After a steely hour of courtroom negotiation, Droste was granted a residence permit, which would allow him to work until the end of the month.

This scandal had a publicity value. The whole thing, of course, delighted Anita, who was otherwise busy shooting filmed scenes for a nineteenth-century love story *Vienna: City of Songs* and a modern "sensational drama," *Light From the Depths* (which captured her "Astarte" in a dance-hall setting).

On November 30th, a second evening of *Dances of Depravity, Horror, and Ecstasy* filled the Great Konzerthaus-Saal. Droste used this and the earlier success as well as the jewelry store scandal to secure still another "exclusive" contract. This agreement was with Moritz Rosner's Ronacher Theater. Anita and Droste were to receive one million kroner for the month-long engagement. But Droste's legal problems would soon balloon.

When Dr. Rosner went to extend Anita and Droste's Viennese residence permits through the month of December, a police clerk informed him that the Apollo-Theater revue house and the Tarabin cabaret had already petitioned for a similar licence. Droste had evidentially booked "exclusive" engagements with two other variety venues. The cheeky showman calculated that he could fulfill all the dance assignments by craftily shuttling from the theatre to revue-house to nightclub through a staggered evening schedule.

Rosner contacted the International Artists' Union in order to sue for breach of contract. At the main Viennese courthouse, the IAU's attorney, Dr. Moritz Kohn, won an

Illustriertes Wiener Extrablatt,
December 1, 1922

injunction against the dancers. Anita Berber and Sebastian Droste could only appear on Rosner's stage or risk imprisonment. Droste's lawyer, Dr. Stiegland, failed to overturn the ruling.

Meanwhile Berber-Droste's "epoch dance creations" headlined Ben Tiber's Christmas program. Also on the revue roster was Dr. Leopold Thoma's sketch on female criminality, entitled "The Woman," and Fred Marion's mind-reading act along with ten other vaudeville acts. The performances were to take place twice daily on Fridays and Sundays through New Year's.

On December 5th, two police officers and an IAU representative waited by the Apollo-Theater stage door, where they hoped to issue the court order directly to Droste. He avoided

The Two Whom Everyone Talks About, after D'Ora, *Illustriertes Wiener Extrablatt*, December 13, 1922

them by entering a side door. Later that night, the police found Droste and Anita "in each other's arms" in the greenroom, where the decree was delivered to them. Still the brazen pair ignored the arbitrated ultimatum and performed at the Tarabin after midnight.

The following day, Kohn notified the IAU in Berlin and had the dancers thrown out of the organization. The Apollo and the Tarabin were forbidden to employ them. In fact, under the IAU articles, no variety stage on the continent, Britain, or Turkey could hire them for the next two years.

Nach der Vertreibung aus dem Paradiese.

After the Expulsion from Paradise **by Cr. Barteau,** *Illustriertes Wiener Extrablatt,* **December 24, 1922**

One week later, Anita appeared in court, wearing a sexy black dress and her monocle. Her attorney protested the IAU banishment but lost the case after one hour of legal wrangling. Vienna's leading tabloid, the *Illustriertes Wiener Extrablatt,* reported the dispute in detail and pasted two images of "Suicide" on their front page (December 13). Over the pictures was the headline: "The Two Whom Everyone Talks About."

Another reference to the troublesome Berliners appeared in the *Extrablatt's* December 24th edition. It showed an angel chasing Adam and Eve from Paradise. Its caption read,

***Tarabin* by Theodor Zasche**

Eve: "What will we do?" Adam: "We'll get an engagement at the Apollo-Theater as naked dancers."

In the last week in December, Siegfried Geyer broke the Berber-Droste boycott. He hired the two to perform at his Kammerspielen cabaret for a New Year's gala. Two policemen attempted to dissuade the dancers from performing but released them at the last second. Anita was arrested the next night before the Kammerspielen show and spent three days in jail. Rosner withdrew his complaint. Dealing with the outlaw performers was futile. He just wanted them out of his hair. They promised to leave Austria on January 1st.

Droste continued his bad-boy behavior. He conned two German countesses out of 70,000 lire, 200 million kroner, and a cache of valuables. Somehow he talked his way out of prison time when the gendarmes came, and instead was declared *persona non grata*. Anita paid his fine and on January 6th, Droste was put on a Budapest-bound traincar.

For the eighth, ninth, or tenth time, Anita violated the civic injunction; she performed at the Tabarin and later at the Komödienhaus with Adoré Villanyi as her Droste substitute. One evening, prankish spectators set off stink bombs in the packed house. Citing exhaustion, Anita left for a weeklong respite in Venice. Only Geyer believed that she would return and, when she did, the tiny creature caused even more havoc in the Viennese entertainment world.

During the curtain call of an unusually wild performance at the Tabarin, Anita saw Dolli Mainz and her husband, the Generaldirector of the Volksbank, in the audience. Covered in sable, Anita walked up to their loge, drank their champagne, and inquired if the two of them wanted to have sex with her that night. Stupefied, both agreed and followed her back to the greenroom. After pilfering a few closets, Anita took the stately couple to the Garderobe and stuffed jewelry (from the Tarbin's spectators) in their pockets and valises and furs under their coats.

A porter approached the suspicious trio as they were exiting from a stage door leading to a back alley. Blocking their path, he inquired what they were doing. Anita punched the old man in the face and threatened him with a hatpin. He struck back with his fists. The ruckus attracted streetwalkers, Tarabin employees, and the corner patrolmen. When the director of the Tarabin saw what was going on, he immediately fired Anita. Dolli and her husband barely managed to drag the raving dancer away in their limousine.

The next day, two police-lawyers came to Anita's hotel room. She received them in the nude. The men ignored her signature provocation and searched her room for stolen valuables. In a drawer was one of the purses that Droste had taken from the German countesses. An official read Anita a proclamation, which ordered her to leave Vienna and not return for a minimum of five years. Anita looked at the document and ripped it in half. She warned the men that she would use it to wipe her ass before their officious eyes. The lawyers calmly exited. Anita was now formally expelled from Vienna; she had exactly three days to depart.

THE EXPULSION
❧ FROM PARADISE ☙

Droste met Anita at the Budapest train station on January 16th, 1923. The Vienna scandals had been followed closely in the Berlin press. The whole thing was given a wacky spin. They had achieved international notoriety but not for the reasons they hoped. The two married at the end of the month.

On February 1st, Anita and Droste began another engagement at the Budapest Tarabin cabaret. At 3 a.m., four vice police and their boss, Josef Torma, whom a journalist from *Der Tag* maintained was already inebriated, came to witness the felons-*cum*-performers. As soon as Anita stepped on the platform, the drunken Commissioner hurled a champagne ice stand from his loge down at the stage. The bottle hit Anita's body with full force and the ice bucket nicked her partner, Baby Palssy. When the Tarabin waiters hustled the constables out of the cabaret, Torma was quoted as shouting, "She should have known it was coming! I am the Commissioner and this is my turf!"

It was a bad omen.

❧ THE BOOK ☙

Droste had high hopes for the Great Konzerthaus-Saal event. Two months before the concert, he convinced Leo Schidrowitz, a Viennese writer, to publish a companion booklet of Expressionist material related to the evening. Schidrowitz had founded Gloriette-Verlag, a literary art house, the previous year. It had already printed luxurious volumes on Chinese poetry, contemporary "Viennese" novels, Wedekind's *Spring Awakening*, and risqué folk songs. Some of the books in the Gloriette catalog were printed in separate leather, half-leather, and linen bindings. *Die Tänze des Lasters, des Grauen und der Ekstase* (The Dances of Depravity, Horror, and Ecstasy) contained dance-poems and manifestoes by Anita and

Droste, 16 photographs from the D'Ora Studio, eight color sketches by their designer Harry Täuber, three self-portraits by Anita, two line-drawings by Felix Harta, and a humorous essay on the naked dance by the Viennese writer Leopold Wolfgang Rochowanski.

In the Gloriette book, Droste's skills as a writer and editor were apparent. No dance book had given such artistic and literary shape to a mimed event. *Die Tänze des Lasters, des Grauen und der Ekstase* both captured the look, and extended the internal meaning, of the production. It even included descriptions and illustrated materials for dances that were never executed in the November-December 1922 season, like "The Hanged Man and the Depraved Woman," "The Somnambulist and the Convict," and "The Corpse on the Autopsy Table." Täuber's drawing of "The Hanged Man," for instance, showed Droste swinging from a post as Anita laid on her back with her bent legs wide apart. She was catching dead man's ejaculate, the "Devil's spawn."

Unfortunately, the handcrafted book (in one thousand numbered copies) appeared in February 1923, and was too late to be of any commercial assistance for the jettisoned Viennese or Budapest ventures. The short book reviews in Berlin's Galante journals were good but the Anita-Droste personal mishaps overshadowed the intended aesthetic of *Die Tänze des Lasters* as an innovative art object or dance record.

❧ MADNESS ON TOUR ❧

The IAU ban limited Droste and Anita's European venues. They would have to forgo all the major cities and find employment elsewhere. In March, they joined Fred Marion's five-month nightclub excursion to Italy and Yugoslavia.

A smooth-talking stage clairvoyant, Marion had already worked with the tempestuous pair at the Apollo-Theater in December and greatly respected Anita's innate talents. Tiber persuaded the always-overconfident mentalist to take on added responsibility as the dancers' tour manager. Besides organizing the local publicity and arranging accommodations,

Marion had to prevent Droste's and Anita's drug and alcohol consumption from ruining the tour. The German dancers were constantly quarreling and causing problems onstage and off. It was a thankless task.

The mind-reading/naked dance bill started with a month in Naples and a second month-long engagement in Milan. Anita was incorrigible when it came to greeting the press. In Milan, Marion led a half-dozen Italian journalists to Anita's hotel room for an interview. Thoroughly stoned, she invited the anxious reporters into her bedroom and, once ensconced there, she slipped out of her famed sable coat to answer their questions in the nude.

The hotel manager in a Tyrolean resort town was so terrified by Anita's violent outbursts and her husband's combative response that he begged Marion to cart his wards away. The hotel owner even offered to erase the party's considerable bills and pay for their transportation to any other tourist abode. Their nightly and daily bickering was driving away his holiday guests.

Beggar Girl Study **by Fritz Witzel,**
***Die Schönheit*, August 1922**

In Fiume, the trio appeared in a tiny cabaret. The floor space was so small and the place packed so tightly that the dancers could overhear the spectators' whispered chatter. According to Marion's memoir, *In My Mind's Eye* (New York: E.P. Dutton, 1950): "Anita's sharp ears caught an insulting remark muttered by a man seated at a table right on the edge of the floor space. Now, apart from the fact that she was drunk at the time—neither drink nor drug seemed to affect her performance—Anita was extremely near-sighted; in fact her sight was almost as short as her temper. She disregarded the remark at the moment it was made, but marked the position of her verbal critic.

Anita finished her dance and acknowledged the applause. As it died down she strode over to the man sitting in the chair she had marked, and with one tremendous round-house swing of her arm slapped his face with such force that he nearly toppled out of the chair."

But it was the wrong spectator. The mocker had already left his seat and another admiring gentleman had taken his place.

ALONE IN BERLIN

Droste and Anita returned to Berlin in September 1923. Their relationship had deteriorated badly during the Marion tour. Both knew that their great moment had passed. Worse, the two were now hopelessly addicted to cocaine.

In print, Anita's fame continued unabated. A color painting from "The Somnambulist and the Convict" appeared as another *Reigen* cover in September. Simultaneously *Der Junggeselle* and *Shadowland* reprinted D'Ora photographs from the Gloriette book. Very likely these pictorials were Anita's most enduring influence on Berlin's increasingly wild nightlife. Her fashion and cosmetic choices—wearing men's pants and sporting a monocle, affixing a gold chain to one ankle, drawing false eyebrows above her shaved brow, coloring her navel red, snorting drugs in restaurants, publicly exposing her breasts—were widely imitated by the city's young females. Anita was still Germany's number one trendsetter.

Although Droste and Anita made the Hotel Espanade their nest, the two were rarely seen together. Anita returned to her old pre-Droste crowd: Dr. Klapper, Alfred Beierle, Hans M., and Lania. (Just before the November Viennese premiere, Susi began an affair with both the Baroness and Bebi. Three weeks later, she brought them to Berlin.)

The IAU decree effectively stymied the Berlin prospects of the Berber-Droste dance troupe. Anita spent most of her time carousing in nightclubs and wagering at the Six-Day Bicycle Races in the Sportspalast. Occasionally she picked up a foreign tourist for a hard-cash currency transaction and just as quickly converted that money into cocaine. Droste stayed at the Espanade in a comatose drug stupor.

One evening at the Sportspalast, an attractive Viennese girl smiled at the Inflation Queen. Anita did not recognize her; it was Elsie, Gerda's daughter. The two hurried to Anita's hotel room. Droste had passed out on the bed and the substitute mother and the substitute daughter made love on a corner sofa.

One month later, Droste absconded with Anita's jewels and furs. He traded the valuables for cash and booked passage on a New York-bound ocean liner, the *Karlsruhe*. He also purchased clothing that announced his new aristocratic lineage. The dashing conman was now calling himself Baron Sebastian von Droste or Baron Willy Knobloch Droste or some such variant among other lofty appellatives.

Anita was naturally devastated. Dr. Klapper helped her file for divorce. With Droste gone, maybe her art would take on new life, he hoped. Anita's recent sorrows, the recognition of her addictions, her deepening anxieties might provide a kind of inverted emotional springboard. The Madonna from Dresden, more than ever, needed to dance.

CHAPTER FIVE
EXIT BARON VON DROSTE

(1923–1927)

Willy Knobloch was a young man with a variety of artistic gifts but without any single outstanding talent. He was a Romantic without true emotion, an egotist without strength of will, a bohemian out of weakness, a decadent by calculation, and a calculator due to a lack of passion. Herr Willy Knobloch was a true representative of his generation.

—Leo Lania, *Tanz ins Dunkel* (Berlin: Adalbert Schulz, 1929)

Historians of the Inflation era have been uniformly unsympathetic to Sebastian Droste. They saw in him all the charades, confusion, and mocking self-invention of Germany's second-tier Expressionists. Seen from afar, from another century, Droste's work in literature, dance, and theatre was no worse— maybe considerably better—than that of his postwar colleagues.

His presentation of self, however, was always smug, irritatingly feigned, overbearing, ridiculous, bizarrely egocentric, shifting; a smirking dissemblance of authenticity and truth. For those around him, there was no essence, no core, to his protean character. According to Droste's self-definition, that was precisely the point: "Bluffing is everything."

❧ THE EXPRESSIONIST POET ❧

Born Willy Knobloch in 1892, Sebastian Droste came from a life of privilege. His father ran the family business, a silk-stocking factory in Chemnitz. Like other postwar Expressionist writers, Droste went to great lengths to conceal his mercantile and Jewish background. It was bad enough that he had been raised in an upper-middle-class household in Hamburg.

Endowed with a good physique, taste, and musical ability, the teenage Willy escaped his parents' world by enrolling in a local art school, where he excelled in languages, dance, and physical culture. He was a classic dandy, acerbic homosexual, and art snob.

In 1915 Willy's world turned upside down. He was drafted. Nothing is known about his army record but it is probable—based on his poetry—that he served on the Western Front in World War I. His first Expressionist writing appeared in *Der Sturm* in 1919. Altogether, 16 Knobloch-Droste poems and "grotesques" (prose poems) were printed in that august journal between 1919 and 1923. His one known dramatic contribution, "Battle," was published in the Dresden pacifist monthly *Menschen*. Willy's short Expressionist dialogue juxtaposed a Youth's attempt to enlighten the People about the horrors of war with the futile search of a Woman for her Child abandoned in the streets of a nightmarish City.

In August 1919, Willy wrote a series of poems for *Der Sturm* about dancers and dance art. Decadent cabaret shows and the medieval "Dance of Death" were popular themes for both Expressionist artists and writers, but Willy's topic took on a personal and contemporary gloss. In "The Dancer" and "Southern Dances," he described one vivacious, cat-like stage performer as the "ultimate temptress." Her modern dance presentations precipitated a psychic stir in the brains of an unsuspecting audience. It was likely a reference to Anita Berber.

"HERR ORPHEUS,"
❧ THE DANCER OF BEAUTY ☙

The 27-year-old Willy moved to Berlin in the late fall of 1919. He changed his name as well as his calling; the Hamburg newcomer declared himself Sebastian Droste, a nonpareil naked-dancer. Where Droste learned his new trade or got his ideas is unclear but few female cabaret dancers at the time had much traditional training or independent intellectual goals. They only needed to take direction, move rhythmically to the orchestral accompaniment, and have suitable bodies to display. As a tall, smooth-skinned devotee, Droste possessed most of the requirements necessary for the unchallenging environment.

Before New Year's 1920, Celly de Rheidt hired Droste to play the male centerpiece for her *Dance of Beauty* evenings at the Schwartzer Kater on Friedrichstrasse. She retained few male performers and the hunky Droste radiated unconventional charm and lots of dark humor. To the 4/4 timing of cancan fanfare, Celly's newest Orpheus sat on his stage throne and nodded at the nude delights in Jacques Offenbach's underworld paradise. The late-blooming Droste even commanded enough stage presence to mount his own one-man show in March.

Typically Droste needed to explain his work in print. Writing under his *nom de theatre* in *Die Libelle* #12 (December 1920), he spelled out the reasons and meaning of the Naked Dance: it guided the spectator through a silly, constructed Edenic past into another, more truthful existence. In the unshrouded stage-vision, the brush of nude bodies, violent conflict, and harsh sensuality could render the most innocuous of childish fairy tales into a horrifying erotic dreamscape.

Droste seamlessly stepped into the role of an *Ausdruckstanz* choreographer. In the summer of 1921, at the request of Jutta von Collande and Gertrude Zimmermann, he worked with the Münchener Tanzgruppe. By the time he returned to Berlin, de Rheidt's

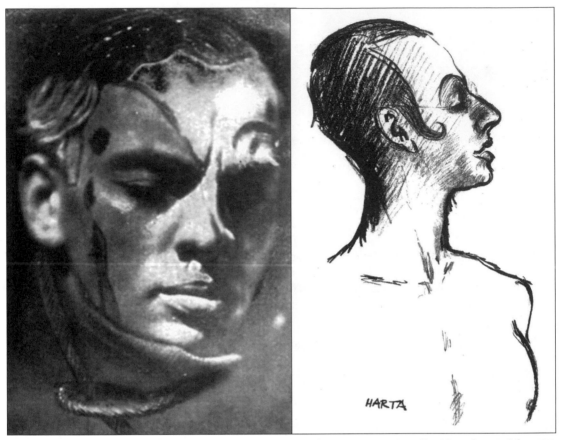

Sebastian Droste photograph by Francis Bruguière, *Das Magazin* #35, July 1927, and Droste drawing by Felix Harta, 1922

"Whip Dance," "Salomé," and the "Harem Ballet" seemed like juvenile versions of his more intensely focused and sexualized productions. The naked Schwartzer Kater numbers, however, were worrisome enough for the vice police. De Rheidt's performances were banned and her husband brought to trial.

It was at this time in the late spring of 1922 that the unemployed Droste attempted to ingratiate himself with Anita Berber. Both had exhausted their solo repertoires. Yet together as a team they had something absolutely novel to contribute to a dance-curious public. It seemed like kismet.

❧ BARON IN THE NEW WORLD ❧

When Droste decided to break from Anita 16 months later and add one more sham identity to his flim-flam persona, there was only one distant Shangri-La he contemplated: New York City. The theatre capital in 1923 was the natural destination for driven European artists and their companies. Jacques Copeau's Theatre du Vieux-Colombier, Max Reinhardt's Deutsches Theater, Konstantin Stanislavsky's Moscow Art Theatre, the Parisian Theatre du Grand Guignol, and G.I. Gurdjieff's Fountainbleu group all scored well during the peak 1922–23 seasons on Broadway. In addition, the children of Europe's dethroned royal families found the New World metropolis far more to their liking and station than their parents' archaic stomping grounds of Paris. In the United States, one could do and be anything one desired. Manhattan, besides earning its reputation as America's financial and cultural center, was also the international city of ambition, an isle of wandering Drostes.

After settling in a tony Park Avenue apartment and carefully scoping his Jazz Age environs, Droste launched a new organization, the International Association Against the Tyranny of Parents. On June 20th, 1924 in a stateroom at the Waldorf-Astoria Hotel, Droste delighted New York City journalists with his screed against parental expectations and restrictions. If a well-brought-up child of means wanted to do something common, like play the saxophone or dance naked, there should be a place for him or her. They should not be treated like "social lepers" or scorned by their unsympathetic elders. Quality painters, musicians, performers could arise from any economic class.

By Droste's side was the junior generation of Europe's prewar aristocracy and a member of America's establishment class: the Princess Alteresco of Romania; Austrian Crown Prince Alexander Dietrichstein; Count Battyany of Hungary; the Turkish Prince Osman Fuad; and Gilbert Kahn, son of the Broadway impresario Otto H. Kahn.

Droste claimed that other centers of his IAATP were already active in the major

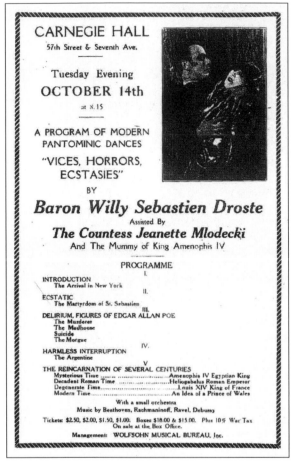

CARNEGIE HALL

57th Street & Seventh Ave.

Tuesday Evening
OCTOBER 14th
at 8.15

A PROGRAM OF MODERN
PANTOMINIC DANCES

**"VICES, HORRORS,
ECSTASIES"**

BY

Baron Willy Sebastien Droste
Assisted By
The Countess Jeanette Mlodecki
And The Mummy of King Amenophis IV

PROGRAMME

I.

INTRODUCTION
    The Arrival in New York

II.

ECSTATIC
    The Martyrdom of St. Sebastien

III.

DELIRIUM, FIGURES OF EDGAR ALLAN POE
    The Murderer
    The Madhouse
    Suicide
    The Morgue

IV.

HARMLESS INTERRUPTION
    The Argentine

V

THE REINCARNATION OF SEVERAL CENTURIES
    Mysterious Time ....Amenophis IV Egyptian King
    Decadent Roman Time ....Heliogabalus Roman Emperor
    Degenerate Time.........................Louis XIV King of France
    Modern Time...............................An Idea of a Prince of Wales

With a small orchestra
Music by Beethoven, Rachmaninoff, Ravel, Debussy

Tickets: $2.50, $2.00, $1.50, $1.00. Boxes $18.00 & $15.00. Plus 10% War Tax
On sale at the Box Office.

Management: WOLFSOHN MUSICAL BUREAU, Inc.

Vices, Horrors, Ecstasies **playbill, 1924**

cities of Europe. Astonishingly, he boasted the sponsorship of Count Albrecht von Bismarck, Otto von Bismarck's grandson; Lord Louis Mountbatten; Prince Pless, a nephew of the Duke of Windsor; Prince Croy of France; the Spanish Infante Don Jaime; and Otto Stinnes, the son of the late German minister, Hugo Stinnes. Further, Droste promised the press corps that monetary support for his elite art league had been secured by Edith Rockefeller McCormick, reportedly America's most naïve philanthropist and notorious female eccentric.

To conclude the nutty conference, Droste read a telegram that had been cabled to the Prince of Wales earlier in the day: "International Association Against Tyranny of Parents organized today. Purpose to assist sons of nobility and old American families to follow their natural artistic talents. We beg you to accept honorary charter membership. Baron Willy Knobloch Droste." (Quoted in *The New York Times*, June 21, 1924.)

The IAATP's first mission, according to the Waldorf-Astoria press release, was to assist its members in an autumn talent showcase that would begin in New York and then travel to London, Paris, Berlin, and end in Rome around Christmastime.

No IAATP performances ever took place. In fact, the organization disappeared from the public record shortly after its grandiose proclamations were issued. Instead Droste starred in a two-person dance evening that opened at Carnegie Hall on October 14th.

Advertised as *Vices, Horrors, Ecstasies: A Program of Modern Pantomimic Dances*,

Droste by Francis Bruguière, 1925

Droste apparently adapted the Viennese Konzerthaus production to American tastes. There was more horror—four dances—and much less ecstasy—one dance. Droste's female partner, the Countess Jeanette Mlodecki, emerged either from his IAATP society or

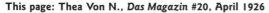

This page: Thea Von N., *Das Magazin* **#20, April 1926**

was another invented noble shill. The single extant photograph ("Suicide") suggests the former. Mlodecki lacked the austere magnetism of Anita and, in the playbill, was listed in a secondary position. Jeanette Mlodecki's name is nowhere to be found in the extensive dance records of the time.

Even the name Sebastian was altered to "Sebastien."

It is clear that Droste counted heavily on the Carnegie Hall evening. In the D.W. Griffith archive at the Museum of Modern Art, there is a handwritten invitation by Droste to the film director with two complimentary tickets inside. (Griffith did not attend the concert and sent his regrets that he did not have a chance to return the tickets.)

Divided into five segments, *Vices* unfolded according to a different narrative logic than the *Dances of Depravity, Horror, and Ecstasy*. For one, Droste played both his and Anita's individual parts. The evening attempted to encompass contemporary and historical time-

Droste by Francis Bruguière, 1925

and-place. The "Introduction" began with "The Arrival in New York." This was followed by the "Ecstatic" part, "The Martyrdom of St. Sebastien." Part Three, entitled "Delirium, Figures of Edgar Allan Poe," contained four dances—"The Murderer," "The Madhouse," "Suicide," and "The Morgue"—of which only two were performed in the Berber production. A comic dance interlude, "The Argentine," in the section labeled "Harmless Interruption," was also a newly added feature. Part Five, "The Reincarnation of Several Centuries," displayed four

The Way by Francis Bruguière, 1925

The Way by Francis Bruguière, 1925

historic personalities as representatives of their depraved epochs: "Amenophis IV" (the old

"Pharaoh's Son" dance), "Heliogabalus Roman Emperor" (Anita's 1919 solo), "Louis XIV

King of France," and "An Idea of a Prince of Wales." The last profile was an obvious citation

to the June IAATP announcement.

Droste's one-shot Carnegie Hall recital elicited no response. Neither the New York

newspapers nor any dance journal reviewed it. A second staging of *Vices* was presented

in December at the intimate St. Michael's Church in the Cloisters at the northernmost

tip of Manhattan. Droste replaced Jeanette Mlodecki with another European aristocrat,

"Thea von N." That live performance was ignored as well. It was to be Droste's last

public offering.

The Way by Francis Bruguière, 1925

⚘ SILVER-SCREEN WANNABE ⚘

Baron Droste moved in various New York social circles. He was rumored to have had love affairs with the Hollywood starlets Gloria Swanson, Mae Murray, and Pola Negri. It was possible. They were all living on the East Coast at the time.

Like much of Broadway and Greenwich Village in the mid-1920s, Droste was ready to plunge into the low medium of silent motion pictures. Its imprimatur was more popular, more glamorous, international, and better paying. That may have been the true motivation for Droste's unctuous correspondence with Griffith, which continued through the spring of 1925.

Droste's only certain cinema connection was with Rosalinde Fuller, John Barrymore's compliant Ophelia in Robert Edmond Jones' 1922 *Hamlet* produced by the Theatre Guild. Directors of both media pursued her. It was probably through her that Droste met the

The Way by Francis Bruguière, 1925

bohemian photographer Francis Bruguière, a San Francisco native and the official portraitist of the Theatre Guild.

Droste tempted Bruguière with a movie idea called *The Way* and the strong possibility of German funding. "Caligarism" still intrigued American artists in 1925, although the 1919 *Cabinet of Dr. Caligari* film was already passé in Europe. The Baron Knobloch himself seemed to have stepped out of a murky Expressionist thriller and his autobiographical storyline traded on the symbolic and melodramatic excesses of the genre: a dreamer who seeks only happiness falls for a young woman, is destroyed by drugs, becomes a circus clown, performs as an Egyptian dancer, achieves absolute power as an Asian despot, and finally withdraws into the life of religion, retiring as a hermit.

Between January and April 1925, Bruguière composed over 60 photographs of *The Way* at his studio on West 49th Street. Although the pictorials were shot in order to interest film producers in the project, Bruguière's spectacular images did more than suggest Droste's Expressionism-by-the-numbers story. Elaborate sets and costumes for *The Way* that closely resembled Harry Täuber's outsized furniture and stage constructions were painstakingly built. Droste and Rosalinde were made up and positioned in artistic poses that few cinema designers had the time or craft to consider. Many of the images were retouched by Bruguière's skillful hand or given multiple exposures.

The photo series of *The Way* was too good to be viewed as mere publicity stills or patently too avant-garde for the prospects of a budding cinematographer. The German UFA studio passed on the Bruguière-Droste film proposal. Droste sent a handful of the stills to *Die Dame* magazine with an article entitled "Photography as an Art: Remarks on Recent Photographs by Francis Bruguière." The piece was published in July.

Exactly two years later, New York's art world marveled at Bruguière's masterpiece. Thirty-five photographs of *The Way* were exhibited at the Art Center. The critics could not think of enough superlatives to describe the serial phantasmagoria. But, by then, Rosalinde Fuller had moved to London and Droste was dead.

⚘ TANTRIK CULT OF NYACK ⚘

Droste spent almost his entire American sojourn in Manhattan with one fascinating exception: he joined a sex cult in upstate New York in the spring of 1925. Founded by Pierre Bernard and his foxy consort Blanche DeVries in 1920, the Tantrik Order was located in South Nyack on the grounds of the former S.R. Bradley estate. The 265-acre property

Droste and Berber rehearsing "Morphine," Atelier Eberth, *Berliner Illustrierte Zeitung*, November 28, 1920

included three mansions, six auxiliary buildings, and a greenhouse. With money from the Vanderbilts, the Goodriches, and other extremely well-heeled devotees, Bernard built a business office, clubhouse, common room, proscenium theatre (the "Throne Room"), lecture hall, commissary, staff housing, indoor swimming pool, seven-acre airport, and an elephant stable. He called his enterprise the Clarkstown County Club.

The Mystic Order of Tantriks not only attracted the sexually adventurous from America's social register but also found adherents among New York's high-octane art crowd and professional set. Experimental composers and conductors (Cyril Scott, Leopold Stokowski), best-selling writers (Hamish McLaurin, Dana Longfellow, Augustus Thomas, Francis Yeats-Brown, William Seabrook, Elsie De Wolf), dancers and actors (Beverly Sitgreaves, Lea Stuart, Lee Tracy), and even the chief architect of the Panama Canal, Henry Goldmark, were charter members. Dr. Frank Crane, America's apostle of self-promotion, Dale Carnegie's foremost inspiration, retired there.

Known in the tabloids as the "Great Oom," Bernard was credited with introducing Tantric and Hatha yoga to the New World. Like his contemporaries Aleister Crowley and G.I. Gurdjieff, with whom he was often compared, the Guru of Nyack blended equal measures of Vedic thought, sexual enlightenment, and modern psychology with hero worship and religious chicanery. Bernard was a master at hypnosis and psychic healing. He met with the press frequently to boast about his new religion of health and sex. No scandal or government official could bring him down.

It was not surprising therefore that Baron Droste von Knobloch gravitated to Nyack and acquired a new occupation: as the choreographer of the Tantrik Order's quirky sex rituals. Dopey dowagers, Sex Magick, Sanskrit salutations, Yogic poses, and now Naked German Dance in Rockland County. New York's yellow press went wild.

❧ THE GURU OF LOVE ☙

Before he blossomed into Pierre Bernard, the "Great Oom" had one of the most ordinary American childhoods and adolescences imaginable. Christened Peter Coons in 1876—or Peter Coon or Perry Baker—he was reared in a small town in Iowa. Young Peter followed in his father's unremarkable footsteps as a barber until his twentieth birthday when he headed west to California. Unable to find work except in the fruit fields and fish canneries, Peter seemed destined for a life of struggle and disappointment. But in the lemon orchards of Lincoln, California, the down-and-out Iowan rubbed shoulders with a real East Indian mystic, Sylvais Hamati. The far-flung swami realized that this was his first American disciple and trained him in the occult arts of his ancient and mysterious land.

Peter never worked as a day laborer again. He transformed into Pierre Bernard, High Tantrik Priest, "soul-charmer," and all-purpose man-god. Shuttling between Tacoma, Portland, San Francisco, and Seattle, the flamboyant yoga teacher set up various clinics and houses of worship. In San Francisco, he ran the Bacchante Club. When his partner claimed that Bernard had hypnotized him into performing licentious acts, the cigar-smoking guru got religion; he incorporated his flock into a Temple of Tantrik. The police raided the joint when a runaway girl was discovered there. Bernard was charged with embezzlement of community funds but confused the court-appointed jury to such a degree that he walked out of the Hall of Justice a free and morally spotless citizen.

At San Francisco's French Hospital, Bernard proved his corporal mastery by simulating a deathly state. Physicians stuck needles in his hirsute arms, which failed to register pain. His auto-entrancement was certified.

Leaving San Francisco before the 1906 earthquake leveled it, Bernard moved northward to Seattle, where he published the *International Journal of the Tantrik Order*. Descriptions of the Order's rituals give us a suggestion of Bernard's Washington State activities: "Tantriks worship the beautiful, the sublime, and sometimes select as an object of concentration a

Droste's Tantrik Ceremony of "Mystic Love" in Nyack,
New York Evening Journal, **March 20, 1926**

beautiful girl of about fifteen years, of fair hair and prepossessing appearance, in the best cloth and decked with the finest jewels."

Unfortunately his parishioners were not as discreet or smooth-tongued as their leader. One was booked for abusing a boy. Bernard changed coasts and landed in Washington Heights in New York City.

In October 1909, the Omnipotent Oom opened a sanitarium in Harlem, where he administered morphine and hypnotic treatments. Six months later, Bernard switched venues; he held court at his Temple of Mystery on West 74th Street. Police, looking for underage girls, found him dozing behind a crystal ball. He was sentenced to 114 days in the Tombs before two girls from the Bronx retracted their charges of kidnapping and child endangerment. The indefatigible sex fiend inaugurated his New York Sanskrit College on Broadway and 87th Street two weeks later. He claimed only men were allowed to enroll.

During World War I, the Loving Guru offered a new patriotic service: "Television

Communication" with soldiers in the field. That got him in all the papers and busted as well. Through Blanche, Bernard made contact with the Vanderbilts and their upper-crust associates. The Tantrik cult now had a home in suburban Nyack. In 1923 Bernard campaigned for public office as a county commissioner. He won. The local papers could not believe it. The Great Oom would not be derailed from his sacred mission.

CEREMONIES OF RESURRECTION ⨂ AND COITUS ⨂

Bernard's Tantrik "love colony" was widely rumored to have been the site of numerous lurid and orgiastic celebrations since its inception. But the stories were, by and large, tabloid hearsay. There were no visuals and few verifiable details.

Blanche DeVries, a former vaudeville "Oriental" dancer and yoga instructor, provided the theory for their unconventional work: "Half the domestic tragedies, three-fourths

Tantrik "Love" Procession, *New York American*, May 15, 1927

of the divorces, many of the nervous breakdowns and not a few suicides and murders in America are due to the inherent ignorance and stupidity of the average Anglo-Saxon man and woman on the subject of love! We will teach them!" (Quoted in the Hearst *New York Evening Journal*, March 20, 1926.)

Besides depositing cash offerings with the Clarkstown Club secretary, prospective initiates had to dislodge the emblems of their old selves. After revealing their innermost secrets to the bald priest-confessor, they were given new names and finally schooled in Kama Sutra-like exercises by Madame DeVries. Only then were the Order's members allowed to participate in its erotic theatricals. The basic formula was to dress the women like queens but treat them like slaves. The young men around them would follow suit.

Bernard and Blanche had a rather limited knowledge of modern theatre and dance, so they imported professionals from New York City to design their tantric ceremonies. That is how Droste came to be hired. What the German baron had to contribute to the Mystic Order became clear on December 20th, 1925. He turned the Throne Room into a Berlin parody of the Satanic Mass.

A Pittsburgh broker, Frederick G. Kay, and his wife decided to celebrate the tenth anniversary of their marriage vows. Droste garbed the couple in wedding attire and had the females in their cortege wear nuns' wimples and robes, covering brilliant and sexy clothing underneath.

Correspondingly, the men donned monkish cloaks and cowls. Everyone carried tall candles or torches in the manner of a medieval religious procession. Behind the celebrants were two coffins, which represented the "bride's" and "bridegroom's" fettered, Victorian past.

In the Throne Room, the wooden coffins were overturned and draped as tables. It was on them that an elaborate banquet was set. Meanwhile the curtain rose on Bernard's stage. Berber-like dancers, in harem and Turkish warrior outfits, ritually dueled with scimitars before the turbaned Omnipotent and a live peacock. The performers enacted the Kays' struggle before they came to Nyack and learned the tantric arts. Mystic Love, in the form of sleek debutantes dressed as Nautch dancers, prevailed.

Uniformed guards kept the press at bay. But even *The New York Times* was able to report on the first part of the ceremony (December 21, 1925). The participatory conclusion, however, was left to the readers' imagination. It was an unforgettable event.

THE MYSTERY MAN
⊱ OF SING-SING ⊰

Back on Park Avenue, to keep body and soul together, Droste had to work many jobs. He acted as a freelance correspondent for several German magazines and newspapers like *Die Dame*, *Das Magazin*, and *B.Z. am Mittag*. Interest in Jazz-Age New York was considerable and Droste enjoyed making himself the rogue-hero of his own reportage.

In April 1926, the hanging of America's first celebrity outlaw, Gerald Chapman, was about to take place. Droste obsessed about the story. Capital punishment in Germany had been excised from its judicial system just as the United States began to mass-produce executions through the electric chair, lethal injections, and firing squad. Also, Chapman's contemptuous cop-killing persona had entered into American folklore. He was the subject of countless pulp biographies and obscene cartoons.

Droste's overidentification with the sophisticated and amiable Chapman seems obvious.

Gerald Chapman in "The Chump," circa 1926

They were Nietzschean twins. Their cynical world views were nearly the same, except only one of them had been arrested and convicted. Also, the nimble-footed Droste realized that he had become progressively ill with little time to live.

Through the Chapman affair, Droste once again made the news. With Baby Green as his accomplice, he talked his way into the spectators' gallery of the execution chamber. After the hanging, the *Daily News* crime photographer took several pictures of Baby Green and Droste by the gravesite. They were tagged as Chapman's clandestine socialite sister and her inscrutable friend, the "Mystery Man of Sing-Sing" (April 6, 1926). Other tabloids went along with the sensational story. It was Knobloch-Droste's final con.

"Chapman Will Be Hanged"

Gerald Chapman has sent out four invitations for his execution. Gerald Chapman is a genius. Gerald Chapman is America's master-criminal.

I have received no invitation. I have already witnessed the electrocutions of three criminals at Sing-Sing. I must see Chapman before he hangs.

It is ten in the morning.

Between midnight and sunrise he will cross the line from life to death—what they call the death-sentence.

Gerald Chapman was America's greatest "hold-up man." He spoke six languages. Despite his unrepentant sarcasm and gruesome logic, he received the ultimate penalty from a unanimous jury. In Italy, he would have been made a dictator.

I telephone Baby Green. Only through her can I get into the execution chamber. "Baby," I say, "there's something exciting going on."

"Well," she answers, "I have to sleep."

"No," I scream.

"I will be there in an hour."

"Wear something dark. Something simple, dark, and tailored. Also bring a black hat."

"God," I hear her little boy's voice saying, "are we going to a funeral?"

"Almost," I reply and hang up.

Droste in New York, József Pécsi, *Das Leben*, April 1927

Around eleven, a car arrives. Baby Green is smoking a little opium pipe. She wears a fur coat. And a black muff with an enormous black crown-hat.

"She is game," I think and kiss her hand.

"Not again, Baron," she says. She stretches out her long legs and puffs on her opium pipe. Next to her chauffeur is a funeral cross with nearly 200 orchids.

We will witness the hanging I think and order the chauffeur, "To Hartford, Connecticut."

The car roars off. It takes almost ten hours.

The sweet fumes from the opium pipe; the gassy exhaust from the limo; the scent from the funeral cross—all this makes my head swirl.

How will we get into the execution chamber? All four invitations from Chapman have been sent to the press. Governor Trumbull has expressively forbidden any strangers to witness this execution.

But we will get into the execution chamber!

—Sebastian Droste, *Das Magazin* #35 (July 1927)

⋙ HOME ⋘

In July 1927, around the time *Das Magazin* article appeared, Droste secretly returned to his parents' home in Hamburg. The tuberculosis contagion that ravaged much of postwar Europe had caught up with him. Droste's singular lifestyle probably exaggerated its debilitating effects. The Expressionist poet-turned-dancer and journalist died a few weeks after docking in the German port. Sebastian Droste, remarkably, had reached the age of 35.

CHAPTER SIX
A CARRION SOUL
(1923–1928)

Her powdered face produced a great effect on my 18-year-old psyche. It was a dark and ugly mask. The severely painted mouth didn't seem to belong to her at all; it was more like a bloody red creation that was conjured up from a makeup case. Her chalky cheeks had a violet shimmer. She prattled on without stop and she lied pathetically. It was clear that she had consumed a lot of cocaine. With a deep raspy voice, she told me of her unbelievable adventures—about animals that she hypnotized, about assassinations she dodged. But the hard mask, her face, remained almost unmoving in the semi-darkness.

—Klaus Mann, "Memories of Anita Berber" (*Die Bühne* #275, 1929)

"THE MOST REMARKABLE SPIRIT"

In the autumn of 1923, the last entertainment season of the Great Inflation, Anita was unusually active. She organized an all-female dance group with six smiley-faced teenage hoofers. Troupe Anita Berber performed at various Friedrichstadt and Berlin West nightspots: the Hotel Adlon Bar, Die Rakete, Der Toppkeller, and, notably, at the Weisse Maus. It had much competition. Although Celly de Rheidt had left the city for the domestic tranquility of Vienna, three separate companies of her former dancers traded on their founder's illustrious name.

Anita and her Girls stayed in a suite at the Hotel Adlon. In the evenings she could be found in the hotel's three-star restaurant. Typically, the elaborately decked-out vamp swilled champagne and smoked compulsively in the no-smoking dining hall. One evening, in Hubert von Meyerinck's humorous

Black Cat **by Franz Masereel, 1922**

recollection, she unbuttoned her fur coat, which slid to the floor, and sat totally naked. While the other guests stared in shocked disbelief, the headwaiter tossed the fur wraps back over Anita as he dragged her chair away from the table. Her stately head high, Berlin's "Countess of Sin" departed, followed by two laughing maidens.

The scene was little more than a pre-show warm-up.

At the Weisse Maus, itinerant salesmen from the provinces paid their $3 admission fee. There they squandered their stipends, savings, and their expense accounts on wine and women and naked dance. At adjoining tables, the chieftains of Berlin criminal associations flashed their wealth and countless Friedrichstrasse hookers showed off their short-haired foreign dates. For the unaccompanied, a girl from Troupe Anita Berber was an obtainable trophy. The dance-captain herself was not for sale. And she made that abundantly clear.

After midnight, the guests were ready for the apocalyptic moment when the blouseless girls pranced up the stage ramp. Anita's girls were powdered in deadly pallid shades and appeared like figures of Death incarnate. But Anita performed with bitter sincerity. Each intrusion annoyed her. She responded to the audience's heckling with show-stopping obscenities and indecent provocations.

When the actor Aribert Wäscher called her a "Top Swine," she leaped over to the obnoxious heckler's table and invited him for a closer examination in her hotel room. On

Weisse Maus

another occasion, according to Henry Marx, she climbed on a tourist's table and urinated down her legs. After these inartistic interludes, she remounted the stage in her veils and headdresses and moved with even greater solemnity.

It was not long before the entire cabaret one night sank into a groundswell of shouting, screams, and laughter. Anita jumped off the stage in fuming rage, grabbed the nearest champagne bottle and smashed it over a businessman's head. She tipped over his table, throwing the chairs to the side. The spectator, a middleweight boxer, struck back at the furious dancer. In the chaos, a waiter attempted to right the boxer's table and chairs. Suddenly there was peace and quiet. Everyone sat down and the dance presentation continued to its savage conclusion.

Peter Sachse, the proprietor of the club, whispered to Fred Hildenbrandt, a young dance reviewer and feuilletonist, "Please speak to Anita and tell her that she should refrain from all such shenanigans. You are from the press and maybe she will listen to you. Tell her that she will be thrown out of the Weisse Maus if this happens one more time."

The next evening, Hildenbrandt went backstage to Anita's dressing room. He found

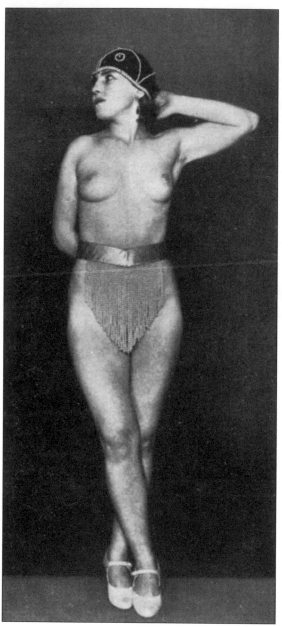

**Dancer from the Anita Berber Troupe
by Fritz Ulbrich, 1923**

her there preoccupied in thought. She looked like a pale teenager seated at her mother's makeup counter. Flung haphazardly on a table was a magnificent diamond wristwatch. With a sigh, Anita asked Hildenbrandt what he wanted to write about. She was about to prepare for her performance but he was welcome to stay.

Greetings From Berlin

She [Anita Berber] began to undress without any embarrassment. No dressing screen. She had a perfect body. Narrow snow-white shoulders, firm breasts with large, dark nipples, her buttocks were perfectly round, her thighs were beautifully arched, the shape of her legs faultless. She was a beauty, and she could have made many men quite crazy. She did that without much effort. Her face was not yet made up. She had enormous black eyes and red-blonde colored hair.

She paced back and forth before me—a living embodiment of sin. I watched her nearly mortified. She affected me beyond any known magic.

I said, "Listen to me, you horrid little thing. You know what you are doing, right? Now stand over there and don't stare at me. Kindly stop making the life of Peter Sachse so miserable. You are always provoking his audiences. I personally don't give a damn. I don't belong here. But you can work in this Lokal only as long as you control your tantrums. You must stop making problems for yourself, that's what I think."

"You aren't a journalist," she said demurely, "you are a psychoanalyst. I know exactly what is wrong with me. I am thoroughly depraved. I snort cocaine. Look, one side of my nose is already destroyed!"

"Sniff at your leisure," I said, "but don't let it ruin your performance."

"My performance," she repeated dreamily. "These evenings are solemn to me. I rehearse with my Girls nonstop. We metamorphose into Death, Sickness, Pregnancy, Syphilis, Madness, Murder, Paralysis, and Suicide, and no one takes us seriously. They gape only at our veils, as if they could see underneath them, the pigs."

I was astonished. These naked dancers executed a serious program about morbid themes and demanded a public, who wanted only erotic amusements, to understand that.

She made herself up in front of a tall mirror, completely naked. She was without any shame. She applied her makeup before me like a guileless child. Suddenly she held her lipstick in mid-air before her chalk-white face, and said, "If you want, you can sleep with me."

I laughed.

She said, "You have nothing to worry about. I am clean. And I make love good."

I said, "I will not sleep with you. I believe that you make love good. But I have a girlfriend, understand? Or don't you understand?"

She just nodded and continued to apply her lipstick and murmured, "Quite the contrary."

She turned to me with her ghostly-white face and finally confessed, "I must dance for these boring lechers and that is what makes me crazy!"

I said, "You must use your fury and convert it into beauty. That is an artistic law from ancient Greece. And remember, Anita, do not try to curb the jeers of those idiots with bottles of champagne."

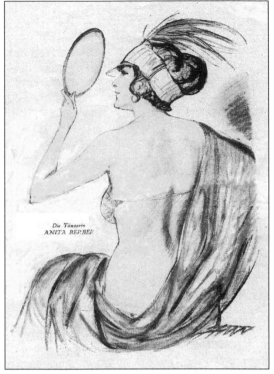

The Dancer Anita Berber by Rolf Niczky,
Der Junggeselle, June 1921

"Right," she answered in an exhausted voice. "Time to clear out."

Anita turned to me once again. Under her painted, hideous mask, she flashed a beatific and enchanting smile. I abandoned her at that moment, dissatisfied with myself. I did not persuade her at all. She was the most remarkable spirit that I ever met in the weird underworld of human sexuality.

—Fred Hildenbrandt (Munich: Ehrenwirth Verlag, 1966)

An hour later, midway into the Troupe presentation, Sachse entered the Weisse Maus. A melee had already erupted. Anita smashed a half-filled wine bottle over the head of an old, bald John. Her Girls screeched approval from the stage and egged on the madwoman to even greater action.

It was Anita's last evening. She was sacked without notice.

❧ OUT OF TIME ☙

The Great Inflation, which had ended in a single day—November 20th, 1923—also marked the collapse of Anita's glorious lifestyle. The alcohol and drugs that sustained her through the Droste era and after had finally taken their toll. As the German nation sobered up and reassessed its cultural future, Anita escaped to the Riviera. Expressionist dance and "Beauty-Evenings" in all their excessive and raw forms were now thought quaint, even innocuous.

In Nice, Anita ran into Dr. Ludwig Levy-Lenz, Hirschfeld's assistant and an expert on female sexuality. Anita confessed that she no longer experienced rushes of corporal desire. Her sensual dances were a perverse masquerade. Inside she was cold, frigid, unfeeling. Lenz attributed Anita's problems to constant cocaine and morphine usage and sheer loneliness. He also thought that these were the very sources of her immoral icy allure. "Many a night she would tell me about her life, and always the same words would come to her lips, 'Why am I unable to love?'" (*Memoirs of a Sexologist*, New York: Cadillac Publishing Co., 1951.)

Lenz advised her to give up her much-loved intoxicants and return home. By Christmas, the decadent vamp, physically wasted and depressed, had moved in back with her mother on Zähringer Strasse. In a few months, she recovered.

Again Anita started performing and causing scandal. The cover story of the February 1, 1924 *Der Pranger* was devoted to Anita's post-New Year's performance at a lesbian celebration on the Himmel und Hölle nightclub stage. The weekly newspaper, for and by Hamburg prostitutes, called Anita "a forgotten genius."

At the Hotel Espanade during the last Sunday in March, Anita danced a more naked version of "Astarte." Tickets were 100 Rentenmarks (1 billion Inflation marks). Rumpelstilzchen described the mood: the puffy hotel clientele drooled like a circling pack of wolves before a farmer's prize sheep.

🌿 THE PASTOR'S SON 🌿

Anita's third and last husband was "a laughing, happy-go-lucky American boy," Henri Châtin-Hoffmann. His father was the renowned founder of the German Evangelical Zion Church of Baltimore. In 1913, the 19-year-old Henri performed for the first time in New York City. Sarah Bernhardt, who saw his modern-dance evening, declared, "Henri begins where the others leave off." It was an accolade he would oft repeat.

Henri came to Berlin. How or why he decided on Germany is not clear. Despite his upbringing, Henri was not fluent in German. He met Baroness Elsa von Freytag-Loringhoven, an eccentric German artist, temporarily living on West 18th Street in Manhattan. He rented a backroom from her in Berlin in December 1923 and began to refer to himself as "Henri the Dancer." Six months later, the effeminate dandy debuted his "First Dance Recital to Modern Music" at the Munich Schausspielhaus. His specialty number was a surreal pantomime, *Three Small Dream Marches* ("March of the Statesman," "The Old-Maid Aunt," and "The Canary"). The weird comic piece was performed to the music of Lord Henry Berners, a British gentleman obsessed with all things avant-garde.

On August 28th, 1924, Henri restaged the same program in Berlin's Blüthner-Saal, the place where Anita had her first success. The cabaret queen not only caught the show but fell madly in love with the

Henri in "Lotus Land," 1931

145

The Candle by Atelier Alex Binder, *Berliner Leben,* **November 1925**

showman. She waited with Klapper in von Nathusius' automobile by the stage door. They sped off with the cheery American.

Two weeks later, Anita and Henri wed. Klapper was the best man at the courtroom ceremony and attempted to revive Henri's memory when he could not recall his father's name. Anita insisted the marriage take place anyway. The baffled judge acceded to the fervent lady's demand. The honeymoon was spent at Klapper's apartment. Anita played the bad housewife, cooking and preparing drugs for Henri. Evenings were given over to nightclubbing and barhopping.

It was a new world for Anita and her foreign husband. One Jägerstrasse strip joint after another was closing down. Revues were suddenly Berlin's hottest attraction.

Henri and Anita performed their first dances together in the Nelson-Revue *Confetti* (October 2, 1924). Nelson, unlike his more naughty competition, attempted to balance his splashy evenings with equal measures of music hall sophistication (à la *Casino de Paris*) and literary Berlin wit. *Confetti* was typical. It was structured on the fantasies of a small-town German teacher who dreams of partaking in the earth's sensual delights. Anita executed a flapper number on top of a school desk and, with Henri, performed a demonic adagio entitled "The Candle."

Confetti closed quickly and the newlyweds were out of work.

Klaus Mann, the 18-year-old son of the Nobel laureate, met Anita and Henri at a Berlin West club shortly after their Nelson-Revue gig. At their table was a suitor, plying them with champagne, but it was uncertain which dancer he was actually pursuing. Around two in the morning, Mann and the suitor delivered the couple to their room at the Hotel Excelsior. Henri fascinated the Mann boy. He realized later that the young man was sweet on both the American and his wife.

That night Klaus listened to Anita's drug-induced chatter. Just her eyes alone, she whined, took one hour to make up properly. Around Anita, Mann intuited, was an icy aura that she had to shatter before it paralyzed her soul. Only sociopathic, manic behavior could keep her sane. The crazy woman had to act out in order to retain her fragile stability.

A few days later, Klaus went to check up on his fallen angels at the hotel. It was late afternoon but Henri was still in bed. Anita had gone to Vienna to shoot her final film, *A Waltz By Strauss*. While Henri rolled lackadaisically under the sheets, his shrewish companion, the Baroness Else, scuttled around the room, mumbling bits of gossip and straightening up the messy surroundings. Henri told his young visitor that he was famished. Klaus asked naïvely why he didn't ring for room service. Henri laughed bitterly; they would not serve him anymore. It was only out of mercy that they let him stay in the establishment. Impulsively Klaus gave the baroness his last five marks. She left promptly for the nearest bar and returned with a Wiener Schnitzel.

With food in his mouth, Henri loosened up and started to speak admiringly of his wife and her singular ability to overcome all known obstacles. "He believed in her, he said laboriously in his hesitating English-German, 'No one can understand Anita.' He sat in bed, with his naked torso exposed. His knees were drawn up, supporting the plate. 'She is wonderful—wonderful beyond all comprehension.'" ("Memories of Anita Berber," *Die Bühne* #275, 1929.)

⍥ THE NEW *HAUPTSTADT* ⍥

Through Henri, Anita attempted in January 1925 to relaunch her stalled career at the upscale Rampe cabaret. For one, she needed to disentangle her old *Dances of Depravity, Horror, and Ecstasy* from the "Beauty-Evenings," which were then being reconsigned to Germany's pile of choreographic amateurism and art junk. A colleague of Anita from her wild Schall und Rauch days, Karl Schnog, even declared that in the year he worked with the diva "she never danced naked." ("Berber-Barbarei," *Das Stachelschwein* #2, February 2, 1925.) That was a stretch.

Not everyone accepted the reinvented, post-Inflation Anita. Alfred Flechtheim, the publisher of the intellectual monthly *Der Querschnitt*, threw a private Fasching-party at his Zoostrasse apartment. He invited Henri, but not his scandal-ridden wife. The hard-partying girl decided to go anyway.

After midnight, Anita arrived at Flechtheim's place in a rush, still wearing cabaret attire from her last dance number. Her costume was a white, virginal Victorian-style dress. The guests in their modern elegant gowns and tuxedos rolled their eyes. No matter. The variety queen was in high spirits. She ordered the pianist to play a Brahms waltz. Henri made an old-fashioned, courtly bow and took her hand. The two professional entertainers waltzed in the center of the room.

First a servant, then Flechtheim, tried to stop the dance. He politely asked Anita to leave the premises, then mockingly reminded her that this was not some vulgar masked ball. Anita screamed threateningly and struck Flechtheim in the face. The publisher was so amazed that he hit her back without thinking. Flechtheim's one hundred guests watched in fright. Again Berber mayhem. Henri led his wife away, repeating in his pidgin German, "People are so bad."

Klaus Mann had every reason to worry about his new outcast friends. Once when a lady on the street pointed a menacing finger at Anita, the enraged celebrity grabbed the woman's hand and nearly bit off the offending digit.

Anita Berber by Becker & Maar

The old Schall und Rauch crew showed a bit more nostalgic sympathy. For a March fundraiser, they advertised the presence of the historic Berlin Dadas, Valeska Gert and Lania, as well as the dance couple Henri and Anita Berber.

The last time Klaus saw his deposed Cinderella was at Hirschfeld's clinic. Henri and Anita had taken up residence in a tiny room there. Anita greeted the boy on her bed. She had no makeup on and looked miserable. The skin on her face was distended, puffy, her blackened eyes swollen beyond recognition. Worse, there was a blue pustule on her neck. The optimistic performer explained her grotesque condition: she had been drinking a little too much with Henri the previous night. Klaus assumed it was something more.

Anita found work at Gustav Heppner's Intimate Theater at the Café Grössenwahn. She danced her current semi-legal addiction, "Absinthe." This was followed by two erotic farces "The Burr" and "Telephone 19-20." The critics' reviews were warm and encouraging.

Classical/Modern Dances **poster by Curt Wild-Wall, 1925**

❧ ABANDONED ❦

At the Künstlerhaus in Stuttgart on April 14th, Henri and Anita inaugurated their first show together, *Classical/Modern Dances*. The hit number, "Shipwrecked," was seen as a confessional pantomime of two lost souls, once adventurous castaways sentenced to abject humiliation, voluntary separation, physical torment, and meaningless death. The pair was evidently rehearsing their future tour.

"Shipwrecked": Anita and Henri are desperate castoffs on a deserted island. A gramophone placed on top of a barrel grinds out dance-hall favorites—ragtime, fox trots, Charleston, German patter songs. The two pass the time shamelessly dancing by themselves. The woman caresses her breasts, plays with her body. The man juggles imaginary balls as he pretends to ignore her, waiting for their inevitable deaths. Self-consciously, he prances around his indecent partner, parading his body and, like her, voluptuously strokes his own skin. Each solo number blends modern choreography with grotesque mime and heartfelt feelings of despair. The cowardly pair keep moving in the firm belief that dance itself will finally kill them and cut short their sorrow. The survivors' vainglorious pilgrimage through life ends on this forsaken island—with broken limbs, torn clothing, hungry, cold, and hopeless. They are sentenced to die without remorse for all their past vulgarities.

In the autumn of 1925, Berlin now seemed like a hostile art environment for all projects and personalities tainted by the Inflation Expressionism. Something more artistically edgy called the "New Objectivity" had replaced it. The existential shrieks to a vast and empty heaven were now replaced by an atmosphere of ironic detachment and mass culture recreation. Berliners had switched gears again. American slapstick comedy, boxing matches, crossword puzzles, Tiller Girls, racial hygiene, paeans to modern technology, and beautification treatments sparked their leisure activities.

Henri and Anita decided to take their *Classical/Modern Dances* to the provinces.

Shipwrecked **by Ernest Schneider, 1925**

They began in Cologne at the beginning of October. A week later in Düsseldorf, Otto Dix, one of the grandees of the New Objectivity movement, painted a haunting portrait of the emaciated and delusional femme fatale. Her high-collared black "Morphine" dress was chromatically transmuted to a terrifyingly intense, fire-engine red—a better match with the dancer's dyed copper crown. Anita's sickly skin tones were masked in arsenic-like applications of grease and powder. Over her aged head was a halo-like helmet.

Dix and his wife, Martha Koch, caught up with the duo in the spa town of Wiesbaden. During a midnight *Bummel*, Martha saw another side of the former starlet. "Someone would approach her, and she would say '200 marks.' I didn't find that so very awful. She had to earn money somehow. She had to cover the costs of the expensive costumes that she wore for her performances as a dancer. She couldn't earn very much from that. She was just so charming, so sweet, simple, totally natural and delightful." (Quoted from Eva Kracher, *Dix: 1891–1969*

Anita Berber Does Housework by Stefan Lorant,
Das Magazin #20, April 1926

His Life and Works, Cologne: Benedikt Taschen, 1988.)

After Wiesbaden, Breslau, and Leipzig, the *Classical/Modern Dances* program was mounted at the Sekt-Pavilion in Prague. In the middle of a dance, a drunken spectator ordered Anita to strip to the flesh. A major brawl ensued. Defending the honor of his artiste consort, Henri stepped in and was badly injured, losing two teeth in the melee. The local police arrested the culprits. Anita finally understood her place on the European stage was ending.

In April 1926, *Das Magazin* published a different image of the once famed goddess in an unaccustomed domesticity. It showed an underweight Anita wiping down a sink in her filthy Berlin kitchenette. On her face was a look of dread. In the same issue was an article about Droste's successes in New York.

❧ DANCES OF SEX AND ECSTASY ❧

In May, Henri and Anita announced an all-new evening called *Dances of Sex and Ecstasy* for the Alkazar Hamburg nightclub. Among the "new" features was a reconceived version of the "Morphine" dance. Gone was the Renaissance veil and scarf. Here, a less wistful and plain-clothed Anita moved in jerks and disconnected jumps. It was a more truthful display of the narcotic's toxic effect on her body.

Another scandal was reported in June. This one had international repercussions. *Dances of Sex and Ecstasy* was performed in Zagreb, the ersatz capital of the League of

Morphine by Atelier Alex Binder, 1926

Nations-cobbled Kingdom of Yugoslavia. Although Henri had scheduled the production for two nights, he wound up staying in the provincial city for two long months. It was not as if he had underestimated the curiosity of his Croatian public; it was quite the opposite. Most of his time was spent in the corridors of the Palace of Justice and the American embassy. Anita had been arrested and imprisoned.

Morphine **by János Vaszary, *Nyugat*, April 16, 1930**

To amuse herself one Sunday morning, Anita casually strolled around Zagreb's Upper Town. There, in front of the thirteenth-century Gothic cathedral, St. Mark's Church, she spied an entourage of military officers, who had attended the pre-noon mass. The local gawkers stepped back in awe as the high-ranking soldiers sauntered down the ancient steps. Anita did not move.

The leading officer noticed the haughty monocle-wearing femme. Her other eye was practically crossed. In a gentlemanly manner, the man greeted her in Serbo-Croatian. Anita replied in French, "I don't understand your barbaric tongue." Her tone was savage.

The man she insulted was utterly startled. He was Peter II, the King of Yugoslavia. The monarch quickly reverted to French. Their small-talk exchange made the Yugoslav dailies. Anita was tagged the "Serbian Pompadour," a likely secret German agent. (She certainly fit the Hollywood model for one.) Eight days later, Anita Berber was incarcerated. Henri used his American citizenship to get her released. But it took some time and legal wrangling.

After six weeks in jail, the two were escorted to the Hungarian border.

On the train back to Berlin, Anita decided to visit her father, whom she had not seen in almost 20 years. Professor Felix Berber was performing at a Munich concert hall that evening. According to Hans Berber-Credner, his excited half-sister went backstage after the recital. When Anita Berber's name was announced in the greenroom foyer, the elderly violinist maestro turned his back and declined to speak with her. She ran out even before requested to do so. The shocked dancer hung her head and broke down in tears. She cried the entire night.

In Berlin, Henri and Anita were flat-out desperate and without prospects. The diva returned to the cabaret circuit. The vice police were summoned and provided a detailed anatomical report, dated August 9, on her shameless exhibitionism: "The sexual parts [of Anita Berber], around which the pubic hairs

Felix Berber

seem to have been shaved off, are clearly visible and so are imperfectly covered by the hand between the thighs, that the labia bulge out to the left and right of the hand. The posterior is uncovered." (Quoted in Peter Jelavich, *Berlin Cabaret*, Cambridge, MA: Harvard University Press, 1993.)

Anita and Henri had friends in the Netherlands. The young Dutch composer and pianist Franz Bruinier and his brother, August, invited them to Amsterdam to perform a revue, *The World in Reflection*. It was to be an evening of classical and modern dance. Instead, they appeared at Max van Gelder's Centraal-Theater in October performing mostly new material, including two musical compositions by Cyril Scott. Scott, a devoted follower of Madame Blavatsky, was a member of Pierre Bernard's Tantrik Order as well and resided at the Clarkstown County Club at the time the Anita-Henri Amsterdam matinee was staged. He was long considered Great Britain's Igor Stravinsky and the founding father of modern English music, and was among the first serious composers to utilize Celtic melodies and Vedic mythology. Scott's impressionistic pieces were inspired by dark occult themes and Orientalia.

The World in Reflection included:

1) "Legend of Dagobah": Two creatures from the Theosophical pantheon, the Spaniel-King (Henri) and his sister, Dagobah (Anita), enter a throne room. Cyril Scott's "Lullaby"

Legend of Dagobah by Atelier Alex Binder, 1925

establishes both the Arthurian locale and a sense of the fantastic anthromorphic story that will unfold. The sad-eyed canine monarch stands on a pedestal and orders his lesser sibling to amuse him. Dagobah acts out a demure pantomime. The King is taken with Dagobah's touching performance and becomes enthralled by her beauty. Dagobah changes her strategy; her dance turns erotic, taunting, provocative. She pushes her brother off his royal pedestal and he crawls at her feet. Dagobah lifts up her shapely hoof and submissively the King begs to kiss it. The sprightly femme fatale flashes a poodle-like grimace.

2) "March Opus 33": Henri performs this Sergei Prokofiev dance standby in an elegant, traditional style.

3) "Morphine": Most likely this substituted for "Etude Opus 2, No 1" by Alexander Scriabin indicated in the playbill. Its dark atmospheric display and pantomimic precession was the most praised item of the evening. The music was by Spoliansky.

4) "Arabesque Duet": Henri and Anita's choreography respectfully follows Debussy's modernist score. Her gestures follow the exact tonic and rhythmic pattern of the musical Arabesque: Debussy's halves equal her half-steps, the eighth notes register as eighths. Anita's hands and arms move in counterpoint to her legs. Her upper torso responds to the first theme, while her legs dynamically mark the second. Anita's head accentuates the *sforzzata* and the *tenuta*. With *crescendos* forward and up, *decrescendos* jerked backward and down, her body

magically extends its visible line displaying her confidence and the bright qualities of the piece. Henri and Anita move in perfect balance.

5) "Lotus Land": This allegorical dance is driven by the ritual-like, pseudo-Asian court music by Scott. Anita is seated cross-legged on a carpet; she is a divine Lotus floating on a pond. Her arms open like the sacred flower at dawn. She closes her eyes and places her legs in the camel position. She resembles an erotic bas-relief from the Hindu shrine at Khajuraho. Anita's head is raised in a visionary position; her hips and belly are hidden. The Lotus stands on one foot and remains in an upright pose. Her right arm continues

Anita Berber

Anita Berber by Max Brüning, 1925

to spiral upward; her hand flashes a mudra indicating the Indian sign for beauty. Her arms flutter in graceful undulating movements. Finally, Anita recoils downward as her arms cover her face. It is turning night; the Lotus folds its petals.

6) "Narcissus": Henri incorporates the Romantic Debussy theme with the grace of a divine Greek hero. The beautiful boy enters grief-stricken. He pines for his dead lover Echo. Narcissus searches everywhere for her. But in an imaginary spring, he discovers his own reflection, instead of Echo's face. Narcissus is astonished by his perfect image. He is transformed by it and leaps in excitement. The whirling Narcissus has fallen in love with himself. Blackout.

7) "Salomé, Princess of Judah": A palace guard (Henri) drags Salomé (Anita) before a blood-spattered vessel on the stage. She is covered in a scarlet cloak and crawls around the floor like a whipped dog. Salomé stops before the sacred urn and, with closed eyes, remembers the musty, slaughterhouse smell of Jokhanon the Baptist's blood. Shamelessly she rises in a spiral movement. Her face is contorted in lust. To the music of Richard

Top: "Salomé," by József Pécsi, *Das Leben*, May 1927
Below: "Salomé," by József Pécsi, *Nyugat*, April 16, 1930

Strauss' "Dance of the Seven Veils," the Judean Princess prances across the stage, fluttering a sheath of feathers. She immerses her hands in the pot of Jokhanon's blood. Slowly the sex-obsessed maiden crosses her arms over her stomach, letting the red liquid drip down her genitals and thighs. In ecstatic poses, she staggers forward. But her impure passion is not yet quenched. Salomé holds her royal cape high and disappears inside it. Then she drops the cape and presses her crowned head against the top of the holy vessel. Tetrach's naked daughter triumphantly lies down over Jokhanon's coffin. With her head facing downstage, Salomé propels her belly upwards like a slut as she undulates before the prophet's gory remains.

8) "Three Small Dream Marches": a) Lord Henry Berners' tinny march music signals the Statesman's entrance. A diplomat (Henri) walks with small-disjointed steps. Mostly it is his head and hands that react to Berners' percussive parody of a national anthem. As the music turns militaristic, the Statesman pivots sharply and salutes. He urges his invisible troops onward with his arms. Finally, he gives an ironic nod to an imaginary pile of soldiers killed in battle and good-naturedly joins them. b) The march mutates into a dirge. A wealthy Old-Maid Aunt (Anita) comes to the gravesite. Although she realizes that she must die soon, she revels in the power of her wealth. The

Salomé **by Atelier Alex Binder**

Salomé **by János Vaszary, Nyugat, April 16, 1930**

arrogant old woman giggles. A Boy (Henri) traces her steps. His mouth is twisted in fear but his body is joyful in anticipation of his Aunt's death and the fortune he will inherit. The Old-Maid Aunt hangs herself with a cord and falls into the pile of corpses. c) The Boy exits and returns, holding an imaginary Canary. "A canary has died," he mournfully announces. Neither the Statesman, the Aunt, nor the Canary knows how to live or when to die. The Boy fondles the little bird lovingly but

Old-Maid Aunt March by József Pécsi, 1926

it remains unmoving. In mourning, he gently holds the Canary as if he wanted God to resurrect it. The bird magically flies away. The Boy watches it escape death. He wanders off and returns as a grinning Black Man, a Golliwog. His lips are painted red and his arms and legs hang loose from their joints. The Black Man executes an eccentric, expansive cakewalk. During his high-stepping promenade, a striking black Beast romps about the stage. Suddenly the feckless doll senses the danger behind him. He turns pale and bolts into the wings.

9) "Brahms' Waltz": Anita and Henri's steps parallel the basic 3/4 tempo of Brahms' Waltz. The male dancer in black velvet expresses his changing attitudes of love and devotion through *pas chassés*, side glances, low backward leaps, and depage; the female in an off-white transparent cape follows with *chasse glisse*, stationary leaps, and aggressive en arabesque movements. Her spinning *fouettés* are full of fear and despair,

arising from sexual frustration. The dance is actually about power, the struggle of one sex to conquer the other. Yet Henri radiates female beauty and Anita exudes a kind of male grace. The entire waltz unveils their individual lust for dominance but pathetic need for human companionship.

❧ IN FOREIGN LANDS ❧

Anita and Henri stayed in Amsterdam for a while, and then traveled to Prague and other outlying metropolises, probably Salzburg and Bucharest. Only one thing is certain: they avoided Berlin for more than two years.

In July 1927, Henri made arrangements for a Middle Eastern tour. The bookings were haphazardly conceived. The tour began in Athens, where they played in bars and disreputable holiday resort venues. They managed to survive the better part of the year.

New Year's 1928 was spent in Cairo, the center of Britain's Near Eastern colonial administration. From there, the pair went on to Baghdad. A fancy hotel in Alexandria hired them in the spring. Its management was not particularly pleased with Anita's offstage behavior; she paraded around the dance floor with the local waitresses in her arms.

In cosmopolitan Beirut, Henri and Anita performed at 12 different nightclubs and tourist bars. Seventy miles away in Damascus, Henri forced Anita to give up cognac. She was becoming sicker and Syria had heavier prohibitions against the French intoxicant. By the time they drove over the mountains on the way back to Beirut and camped out under the stars, Anita was nearly comatose.

Anita and Henri, 1926

Henri and Helene by Haas, 1928

She suffered from delirium tremens and spit up mouthfuls of blood. That was when she wasn't hallucinating. Anita's weakened body and spirit were in thorough revolt.

On the night of July 13th, the former Queen of European Dance gave her fans what she thought they wanted, a new piece called the "Dance in White." She entered covered in a diaphanous sheet of white like a great bird. Anita attempted two or three *jeté battus*, then sank slowly to the floor, practically dead.

After being formally diagnosed with an advanced case of galloping tuberculosis, Anita refused to believe the senior physician's pronouncement. She desperately wanted to get back to Berlin.

❧ HOME ❧

The journey home lasted four excruciating months, a race against time. Henri accompanied Anita on a luxury liner to Athens. From there they boarded the Orient Express. But at each stop, Anita needed time to recuperate. In Prague, their funds had vanished. They had spent a year's savings of four thousand marks and Anita's jewelry on the costly transport.

The saucy revue-meister Willy Karzin, Paul Markus, and other loyal associates rattled collection buckets in backstage Berlin. That money would be used to bring the fading starlet back to her home on Zähringer Strasse. The modest amount they raised in the end was sent to Prague for just train fare.

Far too ill to be brought to her mother's apartment, Anita was immediately rushed from the Stettiner railroad station to the Bethanien Hospital in Kreuzberg, a working-class district in Berlin.

A small circle, including Leo Lania, came to cheer up the once exotic beauty. Anita looked like a mere outline of herself: "She was thin as a skeleton; unable to stretch out, she sat with her legs drawn up to her chin. Amid the most hideous pain she coughed out her lungs. Despite her agony, Anita wouldn't believe she was dying. 'If only my legs weren't so ugly! They make me afraid,' she said to me. She smiled and tried to paint a red mouth on her face. Her hands trembled and it cost her a terrible exertion. She had the mask of a mad old hag." (*Today We Are Brothers*. Boston: Houghton Mifflin Co., 1942.)

Henri and Helene by Haas, 1928

Into the hospital bedroom, Lania smuggled in Anita's much-prized religious mementos: her old collection of morphine syringes, Madonna and Jesus statuettes, and a box of good-luck charms. The dying woman began to pray. If her divine pleas failed, there were always the morphine needles.

Anita's health improved unsteadily for a week. Friends and relatives surrounded her sickbed. And the pale princess demanded many things from them. She required a benediction from Friar Johannes Kessler, her Dresden priest. Unfortunately, it was discovered that the old priest had gone abroad. Anita made future plans as well. Her thoughts fixated on an extravagant Italian vacation. She even made a promise to quit drinking alcohol cold turkey. Orangeade would be her new cognac.

On November 10th, the 29-year-old dancer died. That very evening, Henri and his new partner, Helene Schelda, opened a show at the Weidenhof-Casino,

Anita Berber's burial took place four days later at the St. Thomas cemetery in Neukölln. One Friar Schmidt delivered the funeral oration. Willy Karzin followed with an amusing farewell. Despite the downpour, the mood was upbeat and festive. After Anita's corpse was lowered six feet into an earthen pit, Henri and Helene then appeared. Henri groused that he was late because he stopped to pick some white roses.

Berlin's newspapers were late too. Suddenly they remembered what an attraction, what an innovator Anita Berber had been. There was more interest in memorializing her artistic accomplishments and personal peccadilloes than any time since the Great Inflation ended. *Der Film* (November 15, 1928), *Reichsfilmblatt* #46 (November 15, 1928), *Berliner Illustrierte Zeitung* (November 26, 1928), *Musik und Theater* (December 2, 1928), and *Filmbühne* (December 10, 1928) all carried laudatory obits.

Hans Feld, in the *Film-Kurier* (November 13, 1928), wrote that although Anita was condemned as "an incarnation of the perverse," she represented an entire generation. Anita had led the fight between bourgeois parents and their freethinking offspring, protested against the rigidity of authoritarian teachers, embodied the thoughts and desires of an unfettered, liberated world. The details of her life and career could be forgotten but her overall influence could not be so easily put to rest.

Portrait of the Dancer Anita Berber by Otto Dix, 1925. Berber poses in her "Morphine" dance costume.

James Klein's Naked Revue "From A to Z" sheet music cover, 1925

Prostitution film poster by Joachim Rágóczy, 1919

The Shame of the Pharaoh's Daughter—a composite drawing of the film
by Ludwig Lutz Ehrenberger, *Reigen* cover, Winter 1920

Anita Berber as the Whore, contemplating suicide, from the "Cocaine" dance.
Drawing by Harry Täuber, 1922

Sebastian Droste as the dying Saint Sebastian, from the "Martyr" dance.
Drawing by Täuber, 1922

Droste as the Sun God, from the
"Egyptian Prince" dance. Drawing
by Täuber, 1922

Berber as the Anointed Virgin,
from the "Vision" dance.
Drawing by Täuber, 1922

Droste as the Madman escaping from his Demon-Shadow,
from the "Lunatic Asylum" dance. Drawing by Täuber, 1922

Berber slices into Droste in "The Corpse on the Dissecting Table" dance.
Drawing by Täuber, 1922

The Murderess-Anita lies on her back to catch the sperm from the
Hanged One-Droste, from "The Depraved Woman and the Hanged One" dance.
Drawing by Täuber, 1922

Two images of Berber in her "Cocaine" corset-dress. Drawing by Täuber, 1922

CHAPTER SEVEN
RITES OF MOURNING

To see her [Anita Berber] walk down the main staircase of the Adlon from her suite on the second floor was a grand sight—almost worth applauding. She was always dressed, or partly dressed, unconventionally; she was the best-known naked dancer in Europe. Her face was chalk-white, and across it was a crimson line, her lips. We who had seen her and her six girls, most of them teenagers, all dancing stark naked, never suspected until a writer in Berlin later revealed it that Anita sniffed cocaine before every performance. This helped produce an almost incredible wildness rarely if ever before seen in a cabaret or theater.
—George Seldes, *Witness To A Century* (New York: Ballantine, 1987)

"REPRESENTATIVE OF HER GENERATION"

German, Austrian, and international interest in Anita Berber was brief but intense. Anita's eccentricities were supremely newsworthy. Between 1921 and 1924, two dozen features about her life and career appeared on the front pages and in society columns of the illustrated Berlin press, Viennese tabloids, and America's fashion monthlies. The naked dancer put a remarkably pretty face and faultless girlish body on the sensational erotic mania that defined Weimar Germany's Inflation era.

Just a few years later, long after the economic stabilization of the Reichsmark, Anita's devotees were reduced to a tiny handful of European intellectuals—Fred Hildenbrandt, Magnus Hirschfeld, Joe Jencik, Leo Lania, Klaus Mann, Paul Markus, and Werner Suhr—and an equally small base of sycophantic aficionados. In Paris, in New York, in Hollywood, and at home, Marlene Dietrich, Lyda de Putti, Leni Riefenstahl, Dolly Haas, Elisabeth Bergner, and even Lotte Lenya had replaced the Dresden Madonna

Anita by Atelier D'Ora, 1922

as Central Europe's filmic representatives of haughty female sexuality.

Accolades for the grotesquely made-up flapper artiste and her choreographic innovations rapidly took on the trappings of a wistful, schoolboy nostalgia. The demonic Berber was a pioneer in her various chosen fields, to be sure, but time and the New Objectivity had eclipsed her novelty. Expressionist excess and nudity had been seamlessly—and ironically—incorporated into the ever-titillating format of the Berlin revue and the popular culture of the city.

By 1925, the foremost avatar of theatrical scandal, Anita Berber, had been thoroughly eviscerated from public memory and civic discourse.

Only the itinerant Red Front journalist, Leo Lania, and the dance historian Joe Jencik, in linguistically distant Czechoslovakia, attempted to preserve the aesthetic legend during the unsettling four-year interlude between Anita's death at 29 and the Nazi coup. Lania's book *Tanz ins Dunkel: Anita Berber* mythologized her life for a general public still curious about the Inflation's decadent past. Jencik's impressionistic monograph, *Anita Berberová: Studie* (Prague: Terpsichora, 1930), on the other hand, was apparently unknown in Berlin because of its small run and Czech authorship. A translated section of *Anita Berberová*, however, was published one year later in Rudolf von Laban's German dance quarterly, *Schrifttanz*. Jencik's piece "Cocaine—An Attempt at an Analysis of Anita Berber's Dance" became one of the most widely read descriptions of a rapturous *Ausdruckstanz* performance.

"Cocaine—An Attempt at an Analysis of Anita Berber's Dance"

Curtain. On the floor, a nude body in an empty room filled with grey-blue dawn. Everywhere, the majesty of death. Above, below, in front, behind, perhaps even inside the motionless figure. Each detail recalls a time when, hand in hand, she entered the room with an old girlfriend. A room where she had to step over the body of Droste, who, in tortured agony, was lying in a cocaine delirium. The memory of this obscene story, in which her second husband had been the sad hero, is the beginning of one of Anita Berber's earliest creations, *Cocaine.*

Deathly silence and no sign of human will. Obviously the first impact of this horrendous poison paralyzes the body. The soul fights hard to regain its dominance. Tiny spasms of the body take hold of the porcelain-colored limbs, and the unfortunate drugged woman regains consciousness—because the desire for life is indestructible. When she sits up, her muscles sway like the motions of a drawn-out pendulum. Her body contracts into a bizarre coil of flesh with two indescribable slits for eyes and a

Anita in "Cocaine," in *ASA* cover photomontage, June 1931

blood-red orifice for a mouth. Slowly the coil unravels as if an order—between reason and delirium—had been issued.

The dancer stands on her feet without any personality. She is a marionette caught in the cruel suspension between poison and life. Her blood, driven by nature, aimlessly rushes through her veins. The intoxicant, injected by man, hopelessly impedes and obstructs; with brute strength, it penetrates the domain of life's great mystery. Her body appears ridiculous and embarrassingly bloated. Inside it boils, outside it is covered in frost. Imaginary attempts to scream melt away; her terror of the cloudy visions suddenly dissolves. The dancer endangers both herself and the creations of her sick fantasy. The healthy body fiercely battles the poison but the heart finally grows weary, and the wild beast of cocaine addiction strangles its willing victim. The dancer throws herself to the floor. More agony—this time it is like the tender sleep one falls into after having been freed from the bowels of hell.

All this is executed with simple steps and natural, unstylized poses. The attitudes of this dance are tragically broken, and the arabesques are demonically protracted. Her body rotates around its axis, languid, as if filmed in slow motion, then—with the crack of a whip—the supple *port-de-bras* come to an abrupt end, as a sculptor might envision it. Abrupt backward movements of the head are incompatible with her body's equilibrium. The foot positions, mostly in broad fourths, accentuate this idiosyncratic art. Her entire technique follows the dynamics of a dream which, when freed from gravity, shatters her solid corporality into the most refined nuances of agility.

    Cocaine and *Morphine* are Anita Berber's most important and most personal artistic creations—like pathological studies by a famous mime. But a mime who understands the right moment to subordinate himself to the shape of the dance without surrendering to it completely.

—Joe Jencik, Schrifttanz (June 1931)

For the great majority of Berlin's cultural scribes and memoirists writing in the early Thirties, Anita's tragic life and singularly defiant persona belonged to an earlier, more naïve period. Germany had changed so much in a decade that the severe economic and social anxieties of the Inflation era then seemed vaguely archaic, even amusing. And the scenic provocations engineered by Anita and her lovers, the public outrage that followed them everywhere, the exposés of drug use and bizarre midnight orgies in hotel rooms, were pronounced dated, picturesque, almost Wilhelmian. The flamboyant outlaw behavior associated with Inflation divas was no longer cutting-edge stuff. There were new drugs and new sexual possibilities in 1932.

Little did the esteemed columnists or their readers know that Hitler's Third Reich would soon subjugate Anita Berber and all the worlds she engendered. Weimar in its entirety, its addictions, and much of its history would completely disappear.

⧽⧽⧽ POSTSCRIPT ⧼⧼⧼

Felix Berber died on November 2nd, 1930, not long after his daughter passed away. The 60-year-old egotist suffered a sad and bitter death.

Lucie Berber lived on in Berlin and, during World War II, when the cabarets and nightclubs shut down, was hired by a German book company. Later a munitions factory employed her. On February 18th, 1954, Lucie died in poverty. A cousin residing in East Berlin assumed financial responsibility for her funeral.

During the Thirties, Conrad (Connie) Veidt relocated to London and in 1940 to

Hollywood, where he played an assortment of costumed villains, malevolent Nazi chieftains, and a Bernard-like cult leader. His signature ironic delivery and devilish good looks made him a much sought-after character actor in wartime features. His last major role was the Gestapo commandant Major Heinrich Strasser in Michael Curtiz' *Casablanca*.

Rita Sacchetto married a Polish count, dropped her career as a dancer after she was accidentally shot in the foot, and moved to Italy.

Klaus Mann joined his sister, Erika, in Connecticut, and then his father, Thomas, in California, where he worked as a journalist for the U.S. Army. He committed suicide in Cannes in 1949.

Many of Anita's colleagues were Jewish. Those who escaped the Nazi dragnet in 1933 and 1934 generally re-established their careers in Great Britain or America and prospered. Richard Oswald continued to direct in the United States. Lania found work as a magazine journalist and biographer in New York and Washington. Fred Marion confounded British parapsychologists with his clairvoyant act in the mid-Thirties and went on to perform in American radio and television venues similar to the *Ed Sullivan Variety Hour*. Charlotte Berend-Corinth, after settling in Italy and Switzerland, taught painting in New York City. Ludwig Levy-Lenz opened a cosmetic surgery clinic in Cairo.

Forced into exile after Josef Goebbels denounced her as an archetypal Jew, Valeska Gert attempted to resume her dance career in London, Hollywood, and New York but with little success. During the war years, she ran a cabaret in Greenwich Village, where Tennessee Williams worked as a busboy and waiter. In 1947 she returned to Europe, playing the part of old chanteuse and cabaret performer. Fellini cast her in *Juliet of the Spirits* (1965). She died in Germany in 1978.

Magnus Hirschfeld was in Paris at the time of the Hitler takeover. He passed away in the South of France two years later. He failed to remount his Institute outside Germany.

Those Jews who remained in Germany and occupied Europe were dispatched to concentration or labor camps. Few survived the 12-year Reich. Fritz Grünbaum, for instance, died shortly after a suicide attempt in Dachau. His highly esteemed art collection of 400 paintings, many of which he shared with Lucie on Zähringer Strasse, was "Aryanized" in Vienna and later resold to the Leopold Foundation. Grünbaum's surviving relatives are still contesting the Nazi "consignment" of his property and its current status as Austrian state property.

Dora Kallmus (D'Ora) escaped to Paris and died in Vienna in 1963. Her studio and photographs were also Aryanized. The original prints from *Dances of Depravity, Horror, and Ecstasy* were thought lost or destroyed.

Only two people associated with Anita managed to artistically trade on her talents and image—although they saw little reason to credit or refer to her directly. These were Vicki Baum and Henri.

Grand Hotel, 1932

Baum left for Hollywood, piggybacking on the success of her novel and play *Grand Hotel,* that quickly transformed into the 1932 MGM cinematic blockbuster and Oscar winner. The role of the vampish Russian ballerina, Grusinskaya, played by Greta Garbo, was said to be based on Anna Pavlova but her character had many obvious Berberesque features that could not be affixed to the touring Russian artiste. The copper-crowned Grusinskaya was stylish, temperamental, depressed, her career in the skids, and utterly love-lost. Moreover, John Barrymore's lead role of the dashing Baron Felix von Gaigern, a hotel thief whose love and saintly devotion saves Grusinskaya from suicide, had more than passing resemblance to Baron Sebastian von Droste, a real conman and hotel-thief. Even the war-wounded and cynical Dr. Otternschlag seemed to be a reference to Dr. Heinrich Klapper. If anything, *Grand Hotel* played out Anita's fantasy of "The Hanged Man"—without its weird erotic conclusion but with the heroic Baron figure shot during a robbery instead of being lynched by a hell-bent mob.

A ghostwriter edited and compiled Baum's posthumous autobiography, *It Was All Quite Different* (New York: Funk & Wagnalls, 1964). She hinted that Vicki's 1921 novel *The Dances of Ina Raffay* was based on Mary Wigman's life when it clearly portrayed a red-haired Berber type. Very likely the American editor did not even know who the original proto-type of *Grand Hotel's* Grusinskaya was either. Five years after her death, few film critics in Europe or America could identify Anita Berber.

Henri, after two years in Europe, returned to New York City. At the Civic Rep, he performed a much-publicized evening of 13 dances. Two of them were Anita's own solos: "Morphium" and "Salomé." The next year he performed Anita's Indian temple dance "Lotus Land." What happened to Henri the Dancer after 1931 is unknown. His name appeared nowhere in the extensive records of dance experimentation on the New York stage.

Henri in *Wild-West Tango*

❧ BERLIN'S MORALITY TALE ☙

More than five decades after Anita's death, the infatigable reporter-archivist Lothar Fischer in a divided Berlin and the outré filmmaker Rosa von Praunheim revived the story of the forgotten temple goddess from Germany's Golden Age. Fischer's book *Tanz zwischen Rausch und Tod: Anita Berber 1918–1928 in Berlin* (Berlin: Haude & Spener, 1984) added much to growing interest in Berlin's interwar culture. Contemporary feminist writers and lesbian historians in Central Europe, inspired by Fischer's dogged research and von Praunheim's 1988 art-house cine-biography *Anita: Daughter of Vice*, finally embraced and elevated the Weimar starlet into the pantheon of "wild girl" heroines and gender-smashing martyrs.

In 1991, to commemorate the 100th anniversary of Otto Dix's birth, his famous portrait of Anita Berber appeared on a German stamp. Once again, the graphic arts secured a place for Anita that her erotic dances could not.

In the English-speaking world, the acclaimed performance scholars Karl Toepfer in his *Empire of Ecstasy* (Berkeley and Los Angeles: University of California Press, 1997) and Lucinda Jarrett in *Stripping in Time: A History of Erotic Dancing* (London: Pandora, 1997) firmly established Anita Berber as a unique and essential personality in the richly-documented chronicle of modern German dance and its allied, if sometimes marginalized, variety arts.

Over the past 15 years, recreations of Anita Berber's *Dances of Depravity, Horror, and Ecstasy* have been successfully mounted in fantastic interpretations on stages in Utrecht, San Francisco, Paris, and by three different troupes in Berlin.

Maybe it is our imagination. Maybe it is something more. But the German Priestess of Astarte has leaped through historical time and space, over and through human generations, to reveal her perfect body and to touch us once again.

And it is not hard to believe that she is still laughing. Laughing and dancing.

THE DANCES OF DEPRAVITY, HORROR, AND ECSTASY

BY ANITA BERBER AND SEBASTIAN DROSTE

VIENNA: GLORIETTE-VERLAG, 1922

I

TO SEBASTIAN

Wax—gleaming wax

A head—a brocade coat

Wax—

Red—as red as copper and living hair

Sparkling hair like holy snakes and flames

Dead

A million times dead

Decayed

And beautiful—so beautiful

Blood like flowing blood

A silent mouth

Night without stars or moon

Eyelids—so heavy

Snow like cold, burning snow

A throat—and five fingers like blood

Wax like candles

A sacrifice from him

—Anita Berber

DANCE

TO ANITA

Aroused, triumphant desire

Sprung—

Crossed waves

Soft billowing waves

Circling circles, unending circles—

Soft billowing waves become desirous waves

On lonesome thrones sits God—

Tidebreaking, screaming desire

Circle-breaking, yellow-green smiles

Devastating dissolving destroying disappearing

Falling leaves from a sprouting plant

Elated

Singing

Sound—

Joyous melting

Grabbing

Spring—

Dance—

—Sebastian Droste

DANCING AS FORM AND EXPERIENCE
BY SEBASTIAN DROSTE

Form is the expression of inner experience. There was a time when it was uniform. The proverb says: treat everything alike. So form is not uniform. Poetry-music-dance shows us that.

Dance is the last and most sensitive form of expressive possibility for mankind. A trembling moment between growth and decay.

There are dancers who move and dancers who experience. The Russian Ballet is only a dance of steps. Uniform motionless steps. It is art created through intellectual technique. The spirit manifests technique through silent rhythms and makes a pleasant link between technique and spirit. Yet the technique vanquishes the spirit.

Most dancers possess technique with little spirit, without experience, mute. And are therefore destitute, spiritless, dead.

Dance is the last and most sensitive form of human expression. Breathing, radiating.

Anita Berber and I dance the *Dances of Horror, Ecstasy, Depravity*. People cry out against our poster-like titles and throw stones.

Yet form is irrelevant. Because each form is an expression of inner experience. Unconscious experience. Stark experience.

Anita Berber doesn't show lecherous depravity. Anita Berber doesn't calculatingly play with the possibilities of lewd times.

Anita Berber is Depravity. And Horror. Horror and Ecstasy.

Our dances, like "Suicide" and "Murder, Woman, and the Hanged One," are not extortions of finely thought out ideas, but gloomy tormented experience. A surfeit of intense experience in bodily form. The unconscious movement of limbs that follow the holy music of the soul. It obeys a strange inner call which frightens us and rips us apart. The holiest shriek of the deepest ecstasy. The whipped tremors of agitated horror. The lecherous abandon of forbidden vice.

And because this experience is spiritual, explosive, bloody, and complete, it is holy. Holy and true. And we are permitted to dance everything that expresses human suffering.

This is how our dances were created. From Depravity—from Ecstasy and Horror. Not through calculated steps before an empty mirror. Not through choreography or thought or ingenious destruction, but through the holiest, unconscious shrieks from the sound of the strange world.

THE LEGENDS
BY SEBASTIAN DROSTE

The unity of expressiveness in physical form, the most sensitive emotion in pantomimic creation, the combination of movement means form, music, color (decor and lighting). That is the essence of the created legend.

Man sees, Man hears, Man feels—

When a beggar begs, when a sick person cries, when a child screams—

This is all expression. Expression. Human expression.

People rush into theatres and concert halls. They reach for programs and read "Dance." Unconscious merriment. Abandoned grace. Joy. Happiness. Love Is spreading within them. Bacchanal—Butterfly—Spring. Femininity is the final goal of their desires because they want to see dance—lively pious cheerful dancing.

There are basements where horror resides. There are sick people who are covered with lesions. There are prisons where human beings wreak havoc. There are knives, daggers, and poisons.

"Oh" whispers the fat successful man to his neighbor, the meticulously groomed secretary, "What do all these horrible things have in common with dance and music? After all one doesn't go to the concert hall to strain one's nerves." This is why dance records only joy and lust.

There was a time where the king's son gave himself to the people. It was Bassianus Heliogabalus who was a boy but also a woman. He stood on the high steps of his temple dedicating himself to the sun. He turned himself into a God through the ecstasy of his body and was sacrificed as a God through the purity of his body.

The striding of his slender thighs. The taking and giving of his girlish arms. The clinging, the shattering, the clutching, the hovering of his fingers.

The divine quivering of holy ecstasy…

And lo and behold, people fell down on their knees and covered their heads, men screamed and women howled because there was lust inside of them. Lust and sensual desire.

Yet he, Heliogabalus, was God. Unapproachable, holy, and true.

And in all countries of the old worlds, dance was greatest religion because he became the model and frightening image of the people. And he was the last bridge between mankind and God. The holiest vessel. The final flickering…

I am now telling you that the legends of the past and our dances that you will see are both of one body.

PRITZEL-FIGURINES
**DANCED BY ANITA BERBER
AND SEBASTIAN DROSTE
MUSIC BY JAAP KOOL**

Wax figures

Decadence

Degeneration

Small hands

Powdered hips

Slender thighs and fumbling fingers

Gems

Jewels

Gold on naked bodies

Narcissists who soil themselves

Self love

Vain straddling

Fondling and purring

But always glass

Much glass

Cut glass

BYZANTINE WHIP DANCE
**DANCED BY
SEBASTIAN DROSTE
MUSIC BY VOLKMANN**

Howling lust

Motionless rearing

Dogged agony

Shattering of a golden temple

Splintering of rusty king's crowns

Bright red streams of blood

Digging up

Burrowing upward from golden mud

Lashing of all vices

Agony and greed

Hitting and shattering one's body with
    howling laughing lust

COCAINE
DANCED BY ANITA BERBER
MUSIC BY SAINT-SAËNS

A lamp suggesting depravity dominates the table, which offers a symbolic foundation to the desperate whore. Its flickering light serves to draw the eerie shadow of the soul toward the edge of the abyss.

Walls

Table

Shadows and cats

Green eyes

Many eyes

Millions of eyes

Woman

Nervously fluttering desire

Flickering life

Glowing lamp

Dancing Shadow

Tiny Shadow

Huge Shadow

THE SHADOW

Ah—jump over the Shadow

It torments, this Shadow

It devours, this Shadow

What does this Shadow want

Cocaine

Shrieks

Animals

Blood

Alcohol

Pain

Much pain

And eyes

The animals

The mice

The light

This Shadow

The horrifying huge black Shadow

HOLY SEBASTIAN
DANCED BY SEBASTIAN DROSTE
MUSIC BY RACHMANINOFF

Matthias Gruenewald

Mantegna

And the tiny church far from Venice

La chiesa di San Sebastiano und Paolo Veronese

Columns

Arrows

And trees

Slender body

Boyish arms

And small hips bound with hemp ropes

Tortured by arrows and knives

Bleeding wounds

Very blue

And bright green

Twisted excruciating groaning

Resisting hands

And enduring torture

Tears become pearls

Tears

Which are firmer than gems and gold

Nevertheless

Greensilver brocade and soft tassels

Stone him

Murder him

But kiss him

Organ

Beatification

And light

Divine

Bluish

Silver light

Raising sound

And the last cry

Bells…

SUICIDE

DANCED BY ANITA BERBER AND SEBASTIAN DROSTE
MUSIC BY BEETHOVEN

Villers de l'Isle Adam

Edgar Allan Poe

E.T.A. Hoffmann

Hans Heinz Ewers

And 1922

Drawing rooms

Tapestry

Silver lamps

Kandinsky

Chagall

And Picasso

Black silk pajamas

Precious silk pajamas

And silver tassels

Long slender white hands

And well-manicured thin fingers

Tormenting dream

And faint resistance against the world
    and God

Slowly striding along

Sliding from existence into non-existence

Hanging head

And falling soul

Moonlight

And the sonatas of Beethoven

Clouds

Powder

And perfume

Twitching

Straining

Constraint

Shriek

Laughter

Scorn

Mockery

Screams

Air…

Piercing realization

White face

Blue-shadowed eyes

Painted lips

And flaming hair

Pleasure boy and prostitute

Bodiless

Soulless

Naked

Haunting whipped memories

From boy to youth

Last clinging on to father

Mother

Society

Tradition

Convention and position…

And the final passage of images

Shining

And living

The green shimmering sins ascend

The cruel imperious lust

The triumph of death

Lust is death

Sexuality

And torture

The poisonous flower stiffens

Clawing

Spanning of spidery fingers

Spreading out

Throwing out

Temptation of the senses

And that is woman

The poisonous

Greenish

Motioning woman

The woman captures

Lures

Reaches and kills

Because woman is sin

Torture and death

Flutters

Chases

Floats

Hides

Screams

Blossoms

Twitches

Bleeds

Chills

Shimmers

Catches

And watches

He grasps with his bent fingers the rope

around her body

And watches

With his hands he touches

He is killing himself

He has killed himself

And around his dead body, the woman—

symbol of everything evil—

giggles and creeps

And her hands apply makeup to her face

Vanishing sounds

Suicide

Suicide

Suicide…

VISION
DANCED BY ANITA BERBER
MUSIC BY BEETHOVEN

Gothic

Spitzbogen

And glass painting

Michael Wohlgemuth

And Schongauer

Also Schaedel's World Chronicles
   and Meister Franke's altar paintings

Luminous

Conceptive

Virgin Mary

Humbly bending down nun

Comprehensive…

Kind universe…

Rigid wrinkles

Divine head

Ecstatic hands

Far away organ

Trumpets and angel's choirs

Passion Play

Crucifixion

Resurrection

Beatification

All human suffering

All human torture…

Birthgiving mother

Anointed Virgin

Vision

Spitzbogen

Gothic

Mary

THE PHARAOH'S SON
DANCED BY SEBASTIAN DROSTE
TRADITIONAL MUSIC

One hundred thousand slaves

Oppressed

Tortured slaves

Forced labor

Stonebridge

Guard

And punishments

He is enthroned on five thousand high steps

He

The son of Pharaoh

Sunpriest and Sungod

Young Amenophis

Painted like an idol

Made up like a pleasure boy

Decorated like a prostitute

The holy triangle

The Sun
And Ra
His body is powdered in gold
And shimmers like the sun
The sun
Ancient symbol of life
He does not yet hold the pharaoh's
    scepter and whip
He does not yet wear the threefold crown
And yet he is already king and God
There are twenty-four pictures

of the Book of Toth
    in the Temple of Memphis
The twenty-fifth is the Fool
The Fool
Who licks the ass of a dog
It is foolhardy to want to know more than
    what the twenty-four pictures in the
    Temple of Memphis say
Painted in gold and motionless
The Pharaoh's son
And the Sungod

MORPHINE

DANCED BY ANITA BERBER
MUSIC BY SPOLIANSKY

A crystal-piercing cry
A delicate sound
And singing
Poems by Verlaine
And the old culture
Not body
Not flesh
Not womb
Yet creation
Only piercing
Half-hearted
Crystal-clear cry
Venice
And gondolas
Surabaya
And Java

Strange flowers
And greenhouse plants
Painted people
And listless sounding bells
So far
So distant
Merging…
Breathing…
An old baroque chair
Finest damask
But worn-out and torn
And then hands
Hands
Which are like made-up flowers
That grow in empty space
And fill it

They fold
And stretch
And cling
And they desire and demand
The slender
Narrow
Throat of the boy's bloodless head
It is rolling on the floor this head
It stares deathly pale at the cosmic being
And shrieks with scornful laughter
   at the mortal worlds
Poison soars from blue hazy circles
It crawls like snakes
White snakes with silver crowns…
It purrs like panthers
Black
Velvety soft panthers

And it smiles
Like sphinxes
Palely made up
Painted white
Mysteriously smiling sphinxes
It is a painting
This is the Mona Lisa
And there was a Master
He was Leonardo da Vinci
And the deadly yellow-green poison
   covers everything
Yet her cry pierces
Pierces
Like a bird
And the sound clinks and rattles
A baroque chair with hands

THE LUNATIC ASYLUM
DANCED BY SEBASTIAN DROSTE
MUSIC BY RACHMANINOFF

Initially five empty eyes glow at us. They belong to three mad lunatics (the fantasy-lunatic, the erotic-ecstatic, and the idiot) who radiate their ecstatic conditions. This becomes clear to the audience after the appearance of the new inmate. Giving in to the mad influence of his new surroundings, he too becomes a picture of insanity. The colored light, which scatters in the moments of ecstasy, has an inflaming effect.

Shouts and a shrieking lament
Widely spread weeping willows
Dark black lakes and never-ending paths
One path
Only one path

Clawing and ripping trees
Shining and torturous horrors
Whose mother is waving
Whose child is crying
Whose tree is growing

Cave	Incestuous corpses
Dripping	Brother's corpse
Rigid grey cave	Sister's corpse
Laughing bound corpses	God's corpse
Share scornful inflexible limbs	Soft and silent laments
Chaotic eyes grasp	A ring
Hack	A stone
Beat	An amethyst
Hurt	A path
Whip	This path
Bite	This long path
Oh—the path of suffering struggles	This endlessly narrow path
Budding hands	Shuts
Torn shirt	Destruction

ASTARTE
DANCED BY ANITA BERBER
MUSIC BY TSCHAIKOWSKY

Explosion	Thoughtless children
Brother's corpse	
Sister's corpse	There is a Divine Female
God's corpse	She is not woman
Moonsilver	She is not man
Silent silver	She is not animal
Dripping silver	She is not God
Wavy waves	She is Moon
Disappearing like breath	Silver
High above	Dangling dripping silver
Ether	
Haze	Twenty-thousand women in corsets
Moon	Bite each other in ecstatic lust

Five-thousand painted boys

Tear each other apart in mad passion

A brother kills his sister

A child is greedy for blood

All slaves are longing for lashes from a whip

All stallions cry for their mares

Only above them silver is dripping

Moonsilver

Soft and holy silver

Melting

Exhaling

Dissipating

Astarte…

She is wearing the coat of divine dissolution

She holds the crown of divine lust

She is wearing the green sapphire of torture

She is cracking her whip

She is naked

She is shouting

She is dancing

All slaves cringe

All stallions roar

And moonlight drips

Silver glows

And Astarte is smiling

Earth

Altar

Sacrifice

Incense

Sacred whores

Pleasure boys

Madness

Animals

Plants

Lotus flower

The Nile

Astarte is dancing

Shameless cries

Naked

Crown

Sapphire

Hips

She is dancing the Great Dance

Boys are sacrificing themselves

Women prepare suicide

Animals are desecrating themselves

Plants are blooming

Astarte is dancing

She takes the big bowl of lust

Grabs it with trembling fingers

Takes the faces of the boys

The heads of the prostitutes

The tails of the stallions

The petals of the flowers

And she laughs

Laughs and dances

THE NIGHT OF BORGIA
DANCED BY ANITA BERBER
AND SEBASTIAN DROSTE
MUSIC BY RACHMANINOFF

Boticelli

Rome

Gobineau

Caesar and Lucretia

Not only incest

But also sex murder

Not only the hips of his sister

But also the claws of death

The foamy rebirth of ancient Rome

Yet the decorated columns of the spreading

Renaissance

She wears the bonnet of Princess d'Este

She has the bent knee of virgins

From the Palazzo Doria

And yet she is only Lucrecia

Lucrecia

The woman

Red hair

Golden net

Pearl on her forehead

He

He, soon to be Pope

(Do not shake your heads)

With slender naked thighs

With a Florentine silver cap

With a pleaded skirt

And nevertheless murder

What is the use

The professors cry

What happened to history

What sacrilege

What shame

And still lovers

Lucrecia

Caesar

Murder

The Night of Borgia

MURDER, WOMAN, AND HANGED ONE

CAST

THE MURDERESS
THE MURDERED BOY
THE HANGED ONE
THE ACCUSERS
ONE HUNDRED THOUSAND HANGED CORPSES

A. THE EVENT

Panting scream

Shattering trembling

Moaning

Falling

A pale boy nervously touches his thighs

Yellow-green desire

Piercing shrills

The woman kills the boys

Desires

Adoration

Pressing

Touches

Tortures

Bloody cry

Emptiness of the moon

A man screams at it

He sees it

And accuses it

He moans in pain

Deadly terror

Black muted silence

Woman escapes the eyes

Destroyed

Scattered

The man grabs the boys

Corpses

Blond corpses

Horrible man

Piercing cries

From every corner, people pour out

Plunging

Circling winding

Mocking laughing

Throwing stones

Crucifying

The crowd accuses

Mocking destiny points to the guilty,
    who is innocent
Passion play
Tale of woe
The body of the boy
Dull
Whispers
Chirping
The crowd stones the innocent one
The man walks innocently
    on the guiltless path of tortures

B. THE EXPERIENCE

This is the evil room of the Woman
The murdering Woman
The Murderess
The view reveals the roofs of the city
Far vast
Dangling
Hangs the Man
The Man
He stands in the room, the Hanged One
The innocent Man
The Woman moans from burning pain
Shrieks from a bloody soul
Tormented voices accuse
The Hanged One accuses
He screams
And scream
He dangles
Dragging
Winding
And screaming
On the roofs, Horror weighs heavily

And the Woman shrieks
    from the boundaries of her soul
And bloodily murders the snakes
And sees that he is hanging before her
The innocent Man
The tortured one
The Hanged One
Circling roars
Raging lust
Desire
Corpse-desire
And poisonous green fear
The Hanged One is hanging
The Hanged One is dangling
The Hanged One on a bloody gallows
The gallows stands in the room of the
Woman
And mocks the vice of flesh
And the cry of the Woman
Gives birth to power
And she cuts the guiltless rope
    of the Hanged One
He slides to the floor
And leaps to the clouds
He leaps
And bounces
He grins
He laughs
He mocks
He mouths a bright lament
And the Woman searches
    for the shadows of the night
From all the corners leap the Hanged Ones
Sneering corpses
Mocking corpses

Chilling corpses
And they cling
Embrace
The corpses
The mocking corpses
The trembling strut of the Woman
And she climbs the gallows' ladder
To measure her own body
One hundred thousand Hanged Ones
    dance the red Dance of Torture
One hundred thousand Hanged Ones
    spread their skinny legs
And arms
And watch as the corpses crush the Woman
And she lays in noose of the rope

Hovered whimpering
Melting
Fluttering…

The Woman sits animal-like on the floor
The Hanged Ones have disappeared
So have the gallows
And the innocent Hanged One
Only dawn
In fearful rooms
The view reveals the roofs of the city
Far vast
Dangling
The Man hangs
The Man

The innocent Man
The Hanged One
Woman sits silently in agonizing pain
She gently leaps
    into the Dance of the Corpses
The Dance of the gray Hanged Ones
And she sees the Animal crawling
    from the corners
The Animal
The Animal which murders and kills her
And shrieking she leaps
Leaps
And leaping she ends her infinite life…

Still twitching, the man dangles from the noose. Below him the fertile ground produces fresh vitals for the hungry contraption.

MAN AND WOMAN
DANCED BY ANITA BERBER AND SEBASTIAN DROSTE

Only two human beings

Two naked human beings

Man

Woman

And both in cages

Strong stationary cruel cages

There was a song about two king's children

Yet it is full of tears

The Man breaks his cage

Tradition

Society

Vomiting convention

A Dance of Vomit a foolish man once wrote

And he leaped at her

But she is only a cage

Useless effort

Dead

Destroyed

And all convention society
   and tradition dances scornfully
   their evil laughter.

THE SOMNAMBULIST AND THE CONVICT
DANCED BY ANITA BERBER AND SEBASTIAN DROSTE

Prison

Head

The Sleepwalker

And the many numbers

Blue, distant longing

Struggle

Roar

Shout

Broken

THE WOMAN WITH THE SEVEN MASKS

DANCED BY ANITA BERBER AND SEBASTIAN DROSTE

She is orchid

And seven heads

Small wax heads

Sprouting

Tired grasps

Thoughts

Dragging

Circling

And she folded into an orchid

THE CORPSE ON THE DISSECTING TABLE

DANCED BY ANITA BERBER AND SEBASTIAN DROSTE

The ghost-like austerity of the autopsy room is indicated by the broken window and door edge, across from a blood-red bier. The actors' ghostly qualities elevate this scene into the realm of the fantastic.

Corpse

Knife

Corpse

Knife

Light

ANITA BERBER POEMS

ORCHIDS

I came into a garden
The garden was full of orchids
So full so full and heavy
It was blooming, alive, and shaking
I could not pass by the sweet vines
I love them insanely
To me, they are like women and boys
I kiss and devour each and every one
All of them died on my red lips
In my hands
In my sexlessness
Which possesses all sexes
I am as pale as moonsilver

Which smelled like sweet semen
From this sensuous flowerland
The hand came closer and closer—
it was brown
And slender
I was "not" afraid
The fingers choked me
Five red drops fell from my lips
Then
I
Was
Dead
A Brown Man plays with my corpse

LONGING

I long for you
My beautiful brown boy
Your eyes could have killed me
Why were you taken from me my lover
All my being was inside of you
I cannot let go, my heart is ripped
A pain so deep—they call it longing
I want to come to you so I could die
For a glance from the depths of your eyes
For a kiss for a bite from you
Why did they take you away from me
You my lover my eternity
I remain with you and you in my heart
Nothing can separate our eternity

DREAMS

He stared at me and the universe
disappeared—
I dreamt about stones pointed—cold—hard
Birds came—sweet shimmering birds
They carried me—to the flowers
The smell was heavy and so intoxicating
That all my thoughts disappeared
I turned as pale as wax
Only my lips were red like blood
And my eyes became black like night
From the flowers I touched and adored
Came a hand

And if in thousands and thousands of years
A creature appears I'll recognize you
   immediately
Your eyes—your hands
Then it must be forever and without end

SEBASTIAN DROSTE POEMS

THE DISSOLUTE ONE AND THE NAKED ONE

He took the powder puff
   and powdered his slender thighs…
He dyed his eyebrows
And painted his lips…
Then he put a golden chain around his hips
And he dipped his fingers into rosewater

He put on white, silken socks
And he tied them with golden ribbons
   around his shaved legs
And his narrow feet slipped
   into soft suede shoes

He then threw on a dull grey cape
   around his naked body
And put a round beret over his head
   which covered his soft blond hair
And pulled the tip of his hat so it covered
   his left shadowed eye…
Then he took the vial
   of Chevalier d'Orsay water
Loosened the silver-plated stopper

And brushed away the pale powder which
   still covered his lightly colored ears…
He poured a few drops of the amber-colored
   intoxicating water over the narrow
   opening of his wide cape…

Then he took an amethyst
   between his thin fingers
And left the house…

A few badly made-up boys hung around the
Piazza Fontanamorosa shyly disappearing
   when they saw him…
Whores screamed like turkeys from the old
Marchesa Spilla's house…

Light-footedly, he crossed the dark square
And turned, softly swaying his hips,
   into the via Roma…
There sat a few pale looking boys
   in front of the Bar Mangini
   cheering to each other and giggling softly

He quietly took some gin
Mixed with heavy Marsala

And slowly, sip by sip,
    he drank the fragrant drink…
He nodded friendly and went without paying
    over to the Piazza
    of the Teatro Carlo Felice…
And dropped his cape
He stood nakedly in the lonely square
And smilingly showed his
    slender powdered thighs

A cry was heard through the streets
People poured out from all the alleys
And formed a circle of staggering bodies
From the Via XX Settembre,
    a troupe of singing Fascists approached
When they saw the slender boy's body,
    they stopped
And fell to their knees…
From the Church of San Lorenzo,
    an Altarboy appeared
And crying he threw himself
    at the naked one's feet…

Women hid their breasts
And pounded their thighs…

A blind beggar fumbled with his hands
    and screamed
Men shouted and hit the ones
    kneeling before them
And sank to the floor, moaning
    at the same time…
Only the Dissolute One stood smiling
    in the crowd…
He wore a narrow dark coat

And a pair of huge black glasses
His face was powdered white
And his eyes were circled with blue eyeliner
His big red lips glowed like a ruby…

The Naked One fearfully touched his
powdered thighs
And tore the golden chain from his hips

The Dissolute One climbed over
    the bodies of the mob
And slowly approached
    the trembling Naked One…

A moan passed over the crowd
The Altarboy timidly jumped to the side…
The Blind One collapsed groaning…

The Dissolute One calmly walked
    towards the Naked One
Putting his skinny golden powdered fingertips
    around his hips
And he kissed his navel…
The lipstick from his red mouth remained
    on the body of the Naked One
And glowed like the bright sun of midnight
Blinded by these scorching rays
The crowd timidly stepped back
And disappeared into the narrow alleys…

The Dissolute One took the slender neck
    of the trembling Naked One
And constantly smiling, strangled him
    with his delicate fingers.

The amethyst fell from the Naked One
made a soft sound when it hit the earth…
The powder trickled down
    from his trembling body
And the glow in his eyes disappeared…

The Dissolute One strangled him
    with scientific precision
And with a swift cut separated the small head
    from the still trembling body

And he sprinkled powder
    over the bleeding wound

He then took the powdered head
    of the Naked One home
Put it inside a glass baroque casket
And fell to his knees and prayed…

TEMPTATION
TO ANITA

…Slender naked boys' thighs
Straddle countless raptures
Scent rounded, bitter pain
Slender lilies' petals
Slim climbing curls

Breathing winding tempting lust
Dull kisses pressed on tendons
Small white bodies twitch
Cuddling
Lusting
Nakedly naked
Clouds of powder veils of light
Rays and colorful round glasses
Swelling ringing silver-sound
Golden brocade silver tassels

Pendulums
Motionless
Pregnant bodies…
Breaking breasts
Laughing hallows…
Boys' arms forming circles
Pulling immeasurable distances
Looping
Winding
Circle and circle…

BIBLIOGRAPHY

Andritzky, Michael and Thomas Rautenberg (eds.), "Wir Sind Nackt und Nennen Uns Du" (Giessen: Anabas, 1989).

Baum, Vicki, *Tänze der Ina Raffay* (Berlin: Verlag Ullstein, 1921).

Belach, Helga and Wolfgang Jacobsen (eds.), *Richard Oswald, Regisseur und Produzent* (Munich: Text + Kritik, 1990).

Berber, Anita and Sebastian Droste, *Tänze des Lasters, des Grauen und der Ekstase* (Vienna: Gloriette-Verlag, 1922).

Bilder-Lexikon, vol. 2 (Vienna-Leipzig: Verlag für Kulturforschung, 1929).

Berend, Charlotte, *Portfolio: Anita-Berber-Mappe* (Berlin: Gurlitt-Presse, 1919).

Eberstaller, Gerhard, *Ronacher: Ein Theater in Seiner Zeit* (Vienna: Dachs Verlag, 1993).

Ehrenberger, Ludwig Lutz, TÄNZE, *Sechs farbige Drucke* (Berlin: Verlag Ludwig Simon, 1925).

Faber, Monika, *Madame D'Ora. Wien-Paris* (Vienna: Brandstätter, 1983).

Fischer, Lothar, *Tanz zwischen Rausch und Tod: Anita Berber 1918–1928 in Berlin* (Berlin: Haude & Spener, 1984).

Gert, Valeska, *Mein Weg* (Berlin: private printing, 1930).

----------------, *Ich Bin Eine Hexe* (Munich: Schneekluth, 1968).

Giese, Fritz, *Girlkultur* (Munich: Delphin-Verlag, 1925).

Goldmann, Otto, *Nacktheit, Sitte und Gesetz* vol. 1 (Dresden: *Die Schönheit*, 1924).

Haustedt, Birgit, *Wilden Jahren in Berlin* (Berlin: Ebersbach, 1999).

Hildenbrandt, Fred, *...ich soll dich grüssen von Berlin* (Munich: Ehrenwirth Verlag, 1966).

Hirschfeld, Magnus, *Geschlechtkunde* vol. 4 (Stuttgart: Julius Püttmann, 1930).

-----------------------, *Sittengeschichte der Nachkriegzeit* vol. 2 (Leipzig-Vienna, Verlag für Sexualwissenschaft, 1932).

Hösch, Rudolf, *Kabarett von gestern* (Berlin Henschelverlag, 1967).

Jansen, Wolfgang, *Glanzrevuen der Zwanziger Jahren* (Berlin: Hentrich, 1987).

Kool, Jaap, *Tänze und Tanzszenen* (Berlin: Adolph Fürstner, 1920).

Lania, Leo, *Tanz ins Dunkel: Anita Berber, Ein biographischer Roman* (Berlin: Adalbert Schulz Verlag, 1929).

Mann, Klaus, *Auf der Suche Nach Einem Weg* (Berlin: Transmare Verlag, 1931).

Moreck, Curt, *Die Erotik in der Mensche Gesellschaft der Gegenwart* (Dresden: Paul Aretz Verlag, 1928).

----------------, *Käufliche Liebe bei den Kulturvölkern* (Dresden: Paul Aretz Verlag, 1928).

--------------, *Sittengeschichte des Kinos* (Dresden: Paul Aretz Verlag, 1926).

Müller, Hedwig, & Patricia Stöckemann (eds.), "*...jeder Mensch ist ein Tänzer*" (Giessen: Anabas, 1993).

Nikolaus, Paul, *Tänzerinnen* (Munich: Delphin-Verlag, 1919).

Oberzaucher-Schüller, Gunhild (ed.), *Ausdruckstanz* (Wilhelmshaven: Noetzel, 1993).

Oswald, Hans, *Sittengeschichte der Inflation* (Berlin: Neufeld & Henius Verlag, 1931).

"PEM," [Paul Markus] *Heimweh nach dem Kurfürstendamm* (Berlin: Lothar Blanvalet Verlag, 1952).

Peter, Frank-Manuel, *Valeska Gert. Tänzerin, Schauspielerin, Kabarettistin* (Berlin: Fröhlich und Kaufmann, 1985).

Pfeiffer, Herbert, *Berlin Zwanziger Jahre* (Berlin: Rembrandt Verlag, 1961).

Rabenalt, Arthur, *Mimus Eroticus* vol. 1 (Hamburg: Verlag für Kulturforschung, 1965).

Riefenstahl, Leni, *Memoiren* (Munich: Knaus, 1987).

Rieder, Ines, and Diana Voigt, *Heimliches Begehren: Eine Verbotene Liebe in Wien* (Hamburg: Rowolt Taschenbuch Verlag, 2003).

Scott, Franz, *Das Lesbische Weib* (Berlin: Pergamon-Verlag, 1933).

Suhr, Werner, *Der Künstlerische Tanz* (Leipzig: Siegels Musikalienbibliothek, 1922).

----------------, *Nackte Tanz* (Egestorf: Lauer, 1927).

von Meterinck, Hubert, *Meine berühmten Freundinnen* (Dusseldorf: Econ, 1967).

von Schrenck-Notzing, Albert, *Traumtänzerin Magdeleine G.* (Stuttgart: Ferdinand Enke, 1904).

Wenng, Walther, *Das Schiefe Podium* (Berlin: Dr. Eysler & Co., 1922).

Jencik, Joe, *Anita Berberová: Studie* (Prague: Terpsichora, 1930).

-------------, *Tanecnik a snobové* (Prague: Terpsichora, 1931).

Magnin, Emile, *L'Art et l'Hypnose* (Geneva: Edition Atar, 1905).

Allen, John C., *Conrad Veidt: From Caligari to Casablanca* (Pacific Grove, CA: Boxwood Press, 2nd ed., 1993).

Auer, Peter, *Adlon* (Berlin: Wiener Verlag, 1997).

Baum, Vicki, *It Was All Quite Different* (New York: Funk & Wagnalls, 1964).

Enyeart, James, *Bruguière: His Photographs and His Life* (New York: Knopf, 1977).

Farneth, David (ed.), *Lenya the Legend* (Woodstock, NY: Overlook Press, 1998).

Gammel, Irene, *Baroness Elsa* (Cambridge, MA: MIT Press, 2002).

Gordon, Mel, *Erik Jan Hanussen: Hitler's Jewish Clairvoyant* (Los Angeles: Feral House, 2001).

----------------, *Expressionist Texts* (New York: Performing Arts Books, 1987).

----------------, *Voluptuous Panic: The Erotic World of Weimar Berlin* (Los Angeles: Feral House, 2000).

Jarrett, Lucinda, *Stripping in Time: A History of Erotic Dancing* (London: Pandora, 1997).

Jelavich, Peter, *Berlin Cabaret* (Cambridge, MA: Harvard University Press, 1993).

Kracher, Eva, *Dix: 1891–1969 His Life and Works* (Cologne: Benedikt Taschen, 1988). Translated by Doris Linda Jones and Jeremy Gaines.

Landau, Rom, *Seven: An Essay in Confession* (London: Ivor Nicholson & Watson, 1936).

Lania, Leo, *Today We Are Brothers: The Biography of a Generation* (Boston: Houghton-Mifflin Co., 1942). Translated by Ralph Marlowe.

Levy-Lenz, Ludwig, *Memoirs of a Sexologist* (New York: Cadillac Publishing, 1954).

Marion, Frederick, *In My Mind's Eye* (New York: E.P. Dutton, 1950).

McGilligan, Patrick, *Fritz Lang: the Nature of the Beast* (London: Faber & Faber, 1997).

Seabrook, William, *Witchcraft: Its Power in the World Today* (New York: Harcourt, Brace and Co., 1940).

Seldes, George, *Witness to a Century* (New York: Ballantine, 1987).

Soister, John T., *Conrad Veidt on Screen* (Jefferson, NC and London: MacFarland & Co., Inc., 2002).

Toepfer, Karl, *Empire of Ecstasy* (Berkeley and Los Angeles, University of California Press, 1997).

Catalogs

Goodbye to Berlin? 100 Jahre Schwulenbewegung Catalog (Berlin: Verlag Rosa Winkel, 1997).

Houchin, John, *Berlin Cabaret* (New York University: unpublished dissertation, 1978).

Otto Dix Catalog (London, 1992).

Der Rhythmus: Ein Jahrbuch (Dresden: Dalcroze Institut, 1911).

"Sodom Berlin" Catalog (Berlin: Beate Uhse Erotik-Museum, 1998).

Periodicals

Arts and Decoration (December 1925).

Asa #1 (January 1927); #6 (June 1927); #2 (February 1928); #6 (June 1931).

Berliner Illustrierte Zeitung (November 21, 1920; November 26, 1928).

Berliner Leben (January 1, 1924; October 1924; March 1, 1925; November 10, 1925).

Berliner Volkszeitung (May 7, 1919).

Die Bühne 5/211 (1928); 7/275 (1930).

Cinema en Theater (Amsterdam) (Autumn 1926).

The Daily News (New York) (April 7, 1926).

Die Dame #10 (February 15, 1917); #1 (October 15, 1917); #15 (May 15, 1918); #5 (December 15, 1918); #8 (January 30, 1919); #24 (September 30, 1920); #7 (January 15, 1923); #11 (March 15, 1923); #15 (May 15, 1923). #7 (January 15, 1925).

The Dance (April 1930; August 1930).

The Drama Review #180 (Winter 2003).

Die Ehe (January 1930).

Elegante Welt 6/3 (January 31, 1917); 8/24 (June 1919).

Die Fackel #601 (November 1922).

Der Film #49 (December 7, 1918); #47 (November 15, 1928).

Filmbühne 3/10 (December 10, 1928).

Film-Kurier (November 13, 1928).

Illustriertes Wiener Extrablatt (November 24, 1922; December 1, 1922; December 6, 1922; December 8, 1922; December 9, 1922; December 13, 1922; December 24, 1922; December 28, 1922; December 29, 1922).

Das Interessante Blatt (Vienna) (December 28, 1922).

Journal of the History of Sexuality (Spring 1992).

Der Junggeselle #13 (January 1921); #24 (June 1921); #15 (April 1922); #36 (September 1923); #16 (April 1924).

Kain: Zeitschrift für Menschlichkeit (March 1918).

KE Magazin (June 1925).

Kriminal-Magazin #8 (November 1929).

Kritiker (July-August 1924; May 1925).

Das Leben (May 1927).

Das Magazin #2 (October 1924); #19 (March 1926); #20 (April 1926); #35 (July 1927).

Marie Claire (January 1995). [German edition]

Menschen 2/7 (July 1919).

Münchner Neueste Nachrichten (March 16, 1904)

Musik und Theater 3/2 (December 2, 1928).

Neues Wiener Journal (October 4, 1922; October 5, 1922; November 14, 1922; December 28, 1922).

New York American (May 15, 1927).

New York Evening Journal (March 20, 1926).

New York Herald Tribune (October 14, 1924).

New York Times (June 21, 1924; December 21, 1925).

Nyugat (Budapest) #8 (April 16, 1930).

Das Organ der Variete-Welt (October 1918).

Der Pranger (Organ of Hamburg Prostitutes) #4 (February 1, 1924).

Reichsfilmblatt (Berlin) #46 (November 1928).

Reigen (October 1919); (February 1920; May 1920; Winter 1920; May 1921; June 1921; December 1921; March 1923; September 1923).

Revue des Monats (January 1930; November 1931).

Schrifttanz 4/1 (June 1931).

Shadowland (January 1921; May 1923; September 1923).

Sibylle (November 1994).

Stachelschwein 2/2 (February 2, 1924).

Die Standarde (October 25, 1921).

Der Tag (Vienna) (February 2, 1923).

Täglichen Rundschau (January 4, 1923; April 3, 1924).

Town and Country (April 1941).

True (January 1965).

Vanity Fair (October 1921).

Research Archives

Pierre Bernard Archive, Historical Society of Rockland County (Nyack).

D.W. Griffith Collection, Museum of Modern Art (New York).

Erich Kettelhut, "Unpublished Memoirs," Kinemathek Berlin.

Interviews

Interviews with Maria Ley-Piscator and Henry Marx by Mel Gordon (1980 and 1981).

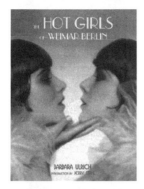

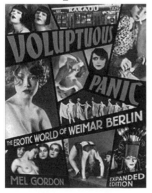